When I Was Young

Stories From My Childhood

Dr. Harry E. Carr
Th.D., Ph.D.

First Printing, April 2002

For additional copies, call or write to:

Shalom Baptist Church
3400 Morgan Road
Orion, MI 48359

(248) 391-0443
Fax: (248) 391-2928

ISBN: 0-9714699-1-1

Library of Congress Control Number:
2002090610

Printed in the United States by:
Morris Publishing
3212 East Highway 30
Kearney, NE 68847
1-800-650-7888

When I Was Young

Stories From My Childhood

Dedication

**This Book is
Affectionately Dedicated
to my Grandson**

**David Michael Carr Jr.
Born May 10, 2001**

**Parents
Dr. David and Lisa Carr**

When I Was Young

Stories From My Childhood

In Memory of
Harley W. Carr
1934-2001

Affectionately called "Jake", he was a brother two years younger than I and a constant companion and buddy during the days of our childhood.

In the months before he went home to heaven, we spent many happy hours on the phone sharing again the events and memories of our childhood years. These are not just the stories of my memory, but of his as well. Ever my admirer and always my friend, he contributed much to the stories in this book. I trust that each story will enrich your memory of Jake.

When I Was Young

Stories From My Childhood

Special Thanks

A Special Thanks To...

"Jake" Harley W. Carr and "Uncle Bill" Alfred E. Carr for helping me with some of the details of the stories.

To my family, ever an encouragement in my writing.
Alberta, my wife of fifty years
Ann and Warren LaTurneau
David and Lisa Carr
Lisa and Gary Montgomery

To Shalom Baptist Church and its ministries, who gave both support and encouragement.

A very special thanks to my secretary and very good friend, Mrs. Crystal (Winegar) Goldsworthy for her tireless efforts in formatting and proofing this book.

When I Was Young

Stories From My Childhood

Table of Contents

When I Was Young

Stories From My Childhood

You Never Outgrow the Days of Growing Up

An Introduction to the Book

You never say goodbye to the days of growing up, they live forever on the pages of your memory. Unexpected childhood friends appear, bringing with them the suns of summer or the snows of winter. Long forgotten, pleasant (as least we hope so) experiences are lived again, and once more you are a barefoot boy or girl wandering down a dusty, country road.

I am pleased to share with you some of the experiences and observations of my childhood. Naturally, some events will require some reconstruction, I will be as honest as possible. Told through the eyes of a youth, the interpretation of events or situations will be sometimes enlarged and other times minimized. Elements of one story may sometimes be related in another. Remember, they are all parts of a whole and some repetition is necessary to tell the new story.

YOU NEVER OUTGROW THE DAYS OF GROWING UP

Some will ask, "Why don't you disclose the names of these persons from long ago?" The very last thing I want to do is to embarrass a family member, a friend, or someone I knew in the early days of my life. Occasionally I will include a brother or sister's name, and of course, Grandpa, Grandma, Dad, and Mom. Other names are recorded in my memory; only a few have managed to totally escape.

You too have stories living in your memory or if you are young, you are now building memories. Your memory will allow you to return to the days of yesteryear, be a child at home, sit on daddy's lap, and let mom dry your tears. For a few moments, you are a kid again, reliving the days of childhood. I invite you not only to share the experience of my childhood and the stories that I heard, but to remember your own. It would be well if you took the time to preserve some of them for your family.

Here and there, I will remember a story told on some cold winter evening around an old stove in the living room. It was rare that we had snack food. There were a few times that we had popcorn, which we had raised in among the regular corn. Grandpa was not a storyteller; for the most part he was quiet. He seldom spoke unless necessary and got on with his thoughts when he did. However, if you listened, there was that rare occasion that he would share the days of his boyhood or tell us a story that had been told to him by his father, whom mother said was just like Grandpa.

I had a rare privilege - I was raised on an old-fashion farm. The only mechanical tools were those that could be pulled by horse or mules or worked by hand. Being raised in a large family, if not in a large house, I was happy in my extended family. My twin uncles, whom we called Bill and Abe, were only eight years older than I, and were not considered to be uncles by me. They were just two older brothers.

I was expected to obey my grandparents just like they were my parents. If in the stories, I mention Grandpa more frequently than others, it was simply because I spent a lot of time with him or with Grandma and Mom. Dad was always working, trying desperately to supplement the meager rations of the home or to buy those items of clothing that you could not buy with the produce of the farm. "Why didn't you sell it off and then you would have money?" You don't understand sharecropping. You live on another man's property, often in a farmhouse. You farmed his land and cared for his cattle, and then you return to him all the cattle and one-third of the crops. You tilled the field, bought the seed, cultivated and harvested the crop, and put one-third into the owners crib. You sowed the field, cut the hay, brought it to the barn, and set aside one-third for the property owner. With Grandpa, the owner never received the bad grain or hay, we took that, he had the best. You had little to sell when only two-thirds belonged to you.

The memories, both pleasant and otherwise, have helped mold our lives. Childhood values are designed for a lifetime when they are not only taught, but are also practiced every day in the home. Gone are the years. I do not wish for the hard times to return. I have had quite enough of them, but it would be great to spend an afternoon in the blacksmith shop, watch a summer thunderstorm from the great hallway of the barn, and smell the exciting aroma from Grandma's kitchen. It would be great to dry my eyes on Grandma's apron, watch Grandpa put a hard case in his place at the blacksmith shop, hear Mommy sing one of the old ballets from the "hollar", and go hunting with Daddy one more time. Or to run with Jake over the hills, hunt frogs in the ponds, or fish on some sunny little creek bank.

It cannot happen, I know for sure, but in my memory I can be a ten year old boy, sighting down the barrel of an old single-shot sixteen gauge at a fox-squirrel clinging to the bark of a tall hickory tree. I can hear the sound as the trigger comes back, feel the full shock of the recoil, and hear Daddy say, "You got him son, let's go home." Swinging my first squirrel by its long, bushy tail, I became the hunter coming home from the hills, for the first of many times.

A Christmas Long Ago

A Short Story by Dr. Harry E. Carr

Christmas was on its way. The weather was cold, but there was no snow. It was a time to be worried. Why? Because Dad had told me that if, there was no snow Santa Claus could not come. The afternoon skies were empty of snow clouds; it didn't look like there would be an early snow this year. Whether you realize it or not, you can make a "worry wart" out of the youngest of boys. There was also another worry; we didn't have a chimney in our house. How would he get in even if he came?

Why making me believe in Santa Claus was important to my parents, I do not know, it was like a religion to them. It was drilled into our heads before, during, and after every Christmas. You simply must believe or Christmas would lose its meaning. I am very afraid that in those days, no one had given me its true meaning beyond the fellow with the red suit, family gathering, and toys. I wrote toys in the plural, but our Christmas consisted of the singular instead of plural when it came to toys. I never remember seeing one manger scene with a baby Jesus in those days, but the fat fellow in the red suit was everywhere.

As skeptical as I was, I had honestly tried hard to believe. At least in front of Mom, I put on my believing face in an attempt to hide all the skepticism of my heart. I had so many reservations about Santa Claus that I could not share with anyone. Why did his signature, placing our names on our toys, look exactly like the handwriting of my Dad? Why was he always poor when we were poor? And how in the world could reindeers fly?

The only thing I was more skeptical about was the Easter Bunny. You know it is sad, but I didn't know what Easter was really about in those days. I only knew that I was suppose to believe in a rabbit that laid colored, boiled hen eggs. Now that might be easy for a city boy to swallow, but pardon me, us old farm boys were just not that dumb. To keep Mom happy, we tried to prepare a place for the rabbits to lay, of course they never laid there. This year I broke the code of silence. I flatly told Jake, my younger brother by two years, that I did not believe in the "Easter Bunny". In fact, I hadn't for two years now. What did Jake do? He reported the "unbeliever" promptly to Mom, who called me in question about this breach of faith and warned me severely about destroying Easter for the other little kids.

I felt terrible about letting Mom down, but I still didn't believe in a rabbit laying hard boiled, colored, hen eggs. I wished at the time that I had known the real meaning of the season, and in some way could have acknowledged the glorious Resurrection of Jesus Christ, our Saviour. I did attend some "sunrise" church services, but it didn't seem important enough to explain to a little boy about the Resurrection of Christ. What opportunities are missed in the early days of our youth?

There was one thing about the Santa Clause that I knew; he didn't have any common sense. For example, in 1939, another one of those lean years, Jake and I jointly received one toy, a metal truck. It had a red cab and a green stake bed. In only a few cases, but especially in this case, it was good to be the oldest and have your name listed first on the name tag of the toy. It gave you seniority and authority at the play place. What a fine choice that old fellow had made this Christmas. You couldn't ask for anything better. This truck was just right for our mining development under the high side of the house.

But on that same nametag, Santa had written the name of my sister Helen. She had been born in April of 1937, the year of the big flood, and she was only two years and nine months old. What in the world would she do with a truck? She couldn't even drive it nor could she make an intelligent engine or gear shifting noise, which we believed necessary in the operation of such a vehicle. It just didn't make sense putting her name on that truck, besides she had her own small doll. That was all she needed, at least, in my thinking.

If this old fellow in the Red Suit was bringing all the gifts free gratis, I never knew why it made any difference whether we had money or not. But invariably December found work scarce, if not non-existent, and I would hear Daddy say, *"There won't be any money so we won't have much of a Christmas this year."* So, what was the big deal? If this Santa fellow were real, he would just take care of it. At least, I hoped.

One should be careful what they whisper in front of children. They listen more than you might think, and in their childish ways they worry, at least I did. In those early years, I don't remember a time when we had much money for Christmas. While this was the truth, and I know it for sure, I certainly didn't need to hear this information, for I had plenty to worry about. The chief among my worries was whether it would snow or not, and since I was skeptical about Santa, why was snow even necessary?

Christmas Eve, regardless of what day of the week it was on, was a time to go to town and dream. We never went to the larger city, just to the county seat. There was one dime store with two little aisles filled with nickel and dime stuff, a few small toys, and occasionally, especially at Christmas, it would have larger items, including trucks, dolls, and wagons.

There were two items that I really wanted to include on my Christmas list, but I did not dare ask for them. One was a big red wagon. We once had a used one and we may have had a very small one once as well, but never the one with the big wheels, and the stake bed with removable sideboards. I would have done almost anything to have a big, red wagon, but they were far too expensive.

I also thought how nice it would be for "Sis", our name for our sister Helen, to have one of the big dolls. But she always seemed to wind up with one that was made of rubber and stared endlessly into space because she couldn't shut her eyes.

A CHRISTMAS LONG AGO

There was always a few nickels or dimes to spend. A quarter was lots of money and a half-dollar was as big as a wagon wheel. It was OK though because you could buy a Pepsi for a nickel and another nickel's worth of candy would last all night. Besides tomorrow there would be some hard candy, soft chocolate drops, peppermint, a few oranges and apples, and if all held together, there would be a dozen tangerines.

We didn't have a fireplace, so our cotton stockings were hung behind the old wood stove in the living room. Again, Santa didn't use much common sense. He dropped those chocolate drops and some of that hard candy down into the toe of those long cotton socks, and the fire did the rest. In the morning, there were chocolate covered hard candies, melted into the fabric of the hosiery. I sure would have enjoyed showing that fellow what a mess he had made the night before.

There was always a lot of tradition based on having good meals at Christmas. All the married children returned home with their families and children, the house was packed out. Granny would cut into one of the hams and fry up great portions for breakfast, along with white gravy and biscuits, fruit or jelly (if any was left), and sorghum molasses. In all the years on the farm, I don't recall eating one baked ham. All meat was either boiled or fried, no one asked if you wanted it that way, the decision was made and that was the way it was.

Lunch and dinner were the same, fried ham or pork shoulder with beans, potatoes, and cornbread. There would be pies, an occasional cake and sometimes Granny would have a jar or two of pickled peaches. Today they are called spiced peaches. They were small cling peaches, canned on the seed using sugar, vinegar, and spices. There were never many of these and the jar was empty all too soon.

In the best of years, we would go into Rosiclare, a nearby town that had a Kroger store, the fresh ground coffee, celery, lettuce, and onions smelled good. They also had the better oranges and tangerines. I don't remember having more than one or two oranges or tangerines, but then I was small and that was enough.

In those years, we sometimes made sorghum taffy in the evenings. We always made it only after the chores of the day were finished. The molasses was boiled until it would ball up in cold water. After it cooled, little hands were rubbed with butter to keep the molasses from sticking, and we pulled and pulled until it became taffy. It was fun pulling the taffy and getting it just right, but far more pleasurable eating it.

Christmas morning was the morning of excitement. What would there be under the tree for us? As meager as it may sound to you, whatever was there was deeply appreciated. I surely hope that I expressed that satisfaction to Mom and Dad, but whoever in the world would put a little girl's name on a truck?

The years have gone but the memory of those simpler days and time has endured. I believe that somehow the experiences of those early years engraved a feeling of gratitude in my soul. I have watched those with an abundance of toys and things, who cannot appreciate even one of them. Poverty isn't all bad. It made us appreciate the joy of giving and the humility of receiving.

The Whinky Whonks of Shawnee "Hollar"

A Short Story by Dr. Harry E. Carr

The Perfect Place for the Story

Mom had her own imagination, and in that imagination there lived a frightful kind of unreal and unnatural being that she referred to as a Whinky Whonk. Was it a ghost, a haunt, the spirit of some nether world? Did it arise in the night and disappear in the day? Were there some places perfectly safe by daylight that might have some spirit being by night?

On the farm where I grew up there was an old abandoned cemetery. Many large farms were like ours with their own little family cemetery. In the years that followed, the family moved away and the distance seemed to far to come back or maybe the memory slowly erased the ties that once bound them to the ones buried there, and the graveyard would gradually become a discarded corner of some field. There were enough of these forgotten places to stir the fertile imagination of a country boy.

In all the years we lived there, I can't remember even one new gravesite. All the graves were old and the gravestones slightly turned this way or that as the bodies and wooden boxes slowly decayed away. Trees grew up through the top of the graves and some even toppled over the gravestones. It must have been a haven for the Whinky Whonks that lived on our farm, or so I thought. I never asked Jake what he thought, maybe because I just didn't want to know.

Mom used these Whinky Whonks to keep the fear of the unknown alive in our minds. It worked well I might add, especially on two boys who were only six and eight years old. You must remember that in those days there wasn't any electricity in the country. The only outside lighting was a kerosene lantern and inside we used kerosene lamps. We were always short of lamps or the kerosene fuel used for their flames. Sometimes it was a thin glass chimney lamp that was broken and had not yet been replaced. At night, darkness reigned supremely, unless it was clear and then the moon could be counted on for its golden glow. I loved those nights when the moon gave its light to the fields and the hills beyond. There would be no Whinky Whonks prowling on this night, you could be sure of that. Now, you have the wrong idea if you think that this always made us stay indoors. There was work to do. The cattle must be fed and milked, the horses must be seen to, and the wood box behind the cook stove and the bin in the living room must be filled. Wood was brought in from the wood yard, and if we just happen to have some coal, it would be located in the northwest corner of the yard and it lay bathed in darkness. You didn't ask questions, and you didn't carry a light unless it was a lantern, which you left in the wood or coal yard until you were finished. Yes that is very true, darkness did reign and it lasted much longer in the winter.

The Origin of the Whinky Whonks

To tell the truth, I never heard anyone else use the name Whinky Whonks before or after Mom. So where did this haunt of the darkness originate? No one that I ever asked knew anything more about it than just the name. Outside of our family, no one else seemed to know where this monster of the imagination originated.

I always thought that maybe it came out of one of the deep hollows of the hills around Mom's home. Perhaps she had heard the story as a little girl. I think, knowing what I do of Mom's parents that one of them may have concocted the demon of the night. Or maybe it was handed down from past generations where it may have represented some sort of fear of the unknown. Grandpa Page, if all that Mom said was true, liked a good ghost story and might have well been the source of Mom's imaginary "Whinky Whonks".

Apparently Grandpa Page loved his little girl and Mom adored her daddy with all her heart. What stories they must have shared around the stove on winter evenings while the wood snapped and hissed in the big stove in the living room! Perhaps here, on a dark stormy night, the Whinky Whonks came from Grandpa's imagination.

What changed Grandpa's relationship with Mom? For some reason Mom never discussed it. She simply said her dad left Shawnee Hollar and found a job on the Ohio and Mississippi River boats as a gambler.

Mom was forced into earning a living for herself, her mother, two younger sisters, and a baby brother. She went to work for a neighboring family. According to Mom she earned enough to feed the family by working on the Asa Cat family farm in the summer and helping around the home and small general store in the winter. It was indeed a hard life for a little girl, and the great love and admiration she had for her father turned into bitterness. She could never understand why he had left her.

The alternative solution to the beginning of the legendary Whinky Whonks may be from Grandma Page. It may be that Grandma, who according to Mom's stories, seemed to live in a land of shadows, superstition, and fear. She may have coined the term Whinky Whonks out of her fear or dread of the unknown, the uncertainty of day by day living or the darkness outside. If I understand correctly what she told me, Grandma had a Cajun heritage through some of her family. It might well be that these legendary monsters known as the Whinky Whonks had been handed down through many generations.

Legends Around the Countryside

There were many legends of ghosts and haunts in and around the countryside. There was always someone who knew someone else who had seen a spook. There were always unexplained shadows or lights in the night, and as usual, any unexplained phenomena just had to be a spirit of something or someone.

Shawnee "Hollar" was no exception to the rule. Some people did not believe in these legends, but a few could tell hair-raising stories about the spooks or ghosts that had been repeated to them from some previous family member. In all this there was deep-rooted superstition, not only in the hollar but also throughout the countryside. Life was hard and Bible knowledge was extremely limited among most. Church services were often conducted once a month, and there was little spiritual training. Superstition clung to many like cheap garments.

Granddad's Stories

Granddad Carr was also full of stories about ghosts and could spin a good yarn about some unusual spook or haunt, especially on a dark, cold, windy, winter night when there was only one dim kerosene lamp flickering in the living room. The old wood stove would have cherry hot spots on the bowl as the fire burned. Sometimes there was popcorn popped in the kitchen on the old wood stove. It was dumped in a large dishpan and shared by all. Once we got our popcorn, we were ready for a story.

Grandpa didn't talk often, so when he talked we listened. His stories were so good that I was often afraid to go to bed. There was no lamp to carry to our room, only the dim lamp that flickered in the bedroom and it was way to far from the bed. To get to our bedroom, we had to cross a hall that led to the outside door and ended in the kitchen just beyond the living room. There were several small holes in the door from the hall into the living room, which someone suggested were probably bullet holes.

Would we meet a ghost on the way to our bedroom? Dimly glowed the oil lamp in the darkness, made even darker by the story. I stirred up the fire in the fireplace until it cast its light in the room long after the kerosene lamp was blown out. What was that eerie glow in the corner? Were the shadows on the wall just shadows or was there really ghost? How impressionable is the young mind, what imagination was stirred up by these stories. If Granddad had known how scared we were, he would have chuckled in his mustache. Grandpa didn't accept weakness or fear. I knew of nothing he feared, whether man or beast. I dared not let him know I was scared.

THE WHINKY WHONKS OF SHAWNEE "HOLLAR"

Although Grandpa Carr's stories were scary, I was always ready for another. Grandpa would reach back into his repertory and out would come another ghost story. One of his favorites was about a farmer that had murdered his wife and burned her body, and hid it in a brush pile. However, according to Grandpa's story, late at night her ghost would appear to her husband in the farmhouse and sometimes she could be seen in the ashes of the brush pile. Finally, her husband could stand no more and confessed his guilt to the sheriff. He was promptly tried, found guilty, and hanged. Grandpa was sure that the haunt or ghost was still in the house or in the edge of the field where the brush pile burned. Now was it a ghost or a troubled conscience?

Inside our bedroom, which consisted of two beds and a fireplace at the end of the room, I would keep the fire burning as bright as possible by building up the wood as high as I could, but then the shadows would dance in eerie fashion on the walls until I covered my heads with the heavy quilts and waited for the break of dawn.

Did Mother Really Believe?

I never really knew how much Mommy really believed in Whinky Whonks or whether she found it a useful tool in keeping us inside. I learned early in life, that if you sang or whistled very loudly the Whinky Whonks would stay away. You can believe me that as a boy, when I walked in the darkest night down a country road, I gave it my loudest if not my best voice.

Please don't ask me what Whinky Whonks looked like, I haven't the faintest idea of their image. They were simply a creature of the night that frightened little boys and I imagine little girls too. Beyond that description fails me. For you see, I never actually saw one neither in my imagination nor in the darkness, and to my knowledge my brother Jake had never saw one either. But in the youth of our lives, in the old farmhouse with no outside lights of any kind, they seemed very real indeed.

We grew up with all the superstitions one can imagine, people swore by them. A bird in the house meant someone was about to die. It was bad luck to rock the rocking chair with no one in it. Never plant a cedar tree because when it gets big enough to shade your grave you will die. The almanac was consulted with more frequency than the Bible or almost any other book, and all too often with more acceptance as truth.

Life was hard in those days, almost everybody worked from sunup to sundown. If they worked at some other job, it wasn't enough. There were gardens in the summer and fall, and pigs or cows to help out with.

Folks mostly depended on family remedies for all sickness as well as smaller personal injuries. There were only three or four doctors in the whole county, and to my knowledge, only one small hospital that was sponsored by the mining industry. I knew only one of the country doctors and had heard of another. Both made house calls and doctored most ailments from their little black bag.

It took a lot of growing up to get rid of some of the superstitions that I knew as a child. Occasionally, I still think of one and smile, but it lost its meaning to me long ago. They were often quite silly; however, it was not wise to tell Mother that. Whinky Whonks lives only in the early days of my childhood and in my memory of those days. They were always more real when Mother said they were there, or when it was dark on lonely roads near small cemeteries or in a place where someone had died.

Whinky Whonks belong to the long ago and the far away, and to the imagination of simpler years and times.

Don't Drive an Angry Boar on Horseback

A Short Story by Dr. Harry E. Carr

Hogs on the Farm

Grandpa had several hogs. Raising pigs was a necessity. A few would be sold, but most were for our own smokehouse. We always killed five to seven hogs. They were raised not only for meat, but also for the lard. What is lard? It is the fat of the hogs that is rendered out by cooking the fat.

In those days, there was no vegetable oil or shorting. Those came during the days of the Second World War. Lard was used in the preparation of almost everything. If it was fried, it was fried in lard. If making bread called for shorting, lard was used. Even the bread pans were first coated with a thin covering of melted lard, and the cake pans were coated with lard as well. All pie or cobbler crusts were made with lard and mixed with flour and water. There certainly isn't any reason why my veins aren't fully clogged with cholesterol. Cooking this way was the only way Granny and Mom knew, and lard was the only thing available to them. In later years neither changed very much, lard was still used and a huge crock of salt set near the stove, from which all things cooking receive a generous portion.

Each year we would put a thousand or more pounds of pork meat in the smokehouse. When the meat was cut into shoulders, hams, and middlings for the smokehouse, there were several pounds of trimming left over. It contained a mixture of lean and some fat. This was set aside with some fat to be made into pork sausage.

Sausage was ground in a hand grinder and mixed with peppers, spices, salt, pepper, and an abundant amount of sage. We didn't buy sage. It was one of the spices that grew in the corner of the garden. There were several others spices growing there as well.

The Peddler

We did buy some spices from traveling peddlers who brought them in their wagons or in the back of their cars. It was always a good day when he came around. Pepper, black and Cayenne, along with cinnamon or cloves were purchased. Occasionally Grandma had a nickel or two and would buy a package or two of butterscotch pudding. I so much enjoyed this little treat. She always fixed it for me before meals, because there was never enough to go around at mealtime.

Making Cracklings

The fat of the hogs was cut and put aside. Later, it would be placed in the black iron kettle in the woodyard and rendered. Most of the pieces, cut into one or two inch slices still had the rind on it. The kettle must be watched closely and stirred often, until it was finished. The fire could not be too hot and boil the grease over into the fire or scorch it. The pieces of rind that were left after the rendering were called cracklings and were much like crisp bacon; however, they were a "little" on the greasy side.

Always after the rendering, Granny or Mom would make shortening bread. It was a corn bread mix with the crackling added in. The bread was somewhat oily, but with a crisp bacon taste. Shortening bread along with buttermilk, beans, and potatoes made up many a supper around hog killing time. Shortening bread is nothing but a memory; however, I can, with the taste of a boy, recall a day long ago when I enjoyed the corner of a pan of shorting bread with a tall glass of buttermilk, cooled in the spring down by the old elm tree at the shop.

The New Butter

Margarine made its appearance during the years of the Second World War. It came in a plastic bag, which was new too; we didn't have plastic things in those days. The margarine was white, and there was a little bubble on the plastic bag that had to be broken and the color worked into the margarine. Honestly, that was the only bag I ever saw on our farm. I think that Grandpa didn't like it and that settled the matter. Plastic would make the day, in years to come, but all we had in those days were utensils of metal, glass, stone, or china and the cooking utensils were all iron, copper, or steel.

Feeding the Hogs

The hog herds were large, and although they did not require great attention, they had to be fed both morning and evening. We didn't have any of those new feeders, and if we had, we wouldn't have had the hog feed to put in them. The hogs were fed corn, table scraps, and on occasion, from a bag of cheap wheat grindings we called "shorts". Shorts smelled good enough to eat. They were mixed with water and dumped into the hog trough.

Five-gallon metal buckets were a premium at our house for feed buckets, whether it was for the pigs or corn for the chickens or the cows. Often times, the corn fed to the chickens was not shelled. The full ear of corn was cut into sections and thrown to the chickens. If there were no "nubbins" (small under-developed ears of corn) then you would have to hack up some corn for the cows that were being milked. Why? Because cows do not have upper teeth and must shell the corn against the hard rigged roof of their mouths, and a full ear could not be easily shelled.

Rings in the Nose

Pigs were ringed. Copper-coated hog rings were clamped in their nose to keep them from rooting under the fences and leaving the pig lot. Sometimes, when the pigs were older, this was quite a chore. They resisted this procedure with all their strength, and they let the whole world know that they had new rings adorning the end of their snouts.

Mr. Hog is Missing

Now, on the occasion of my story, our large male hog, a black and white Poland China, was out. He was a rangy hog and could cover quite a distance. I came through the barn and grabbed a horse to go pig hunting. I made so many mistakes that day that it is a wonder I didn't seriously get hurt. I saddled the little bay horse called Charlie; he was part quarter horse, part Morgan, plus whatever else. But Charlie was extremely high strung; the least of noises set him off. Leaving the barn, I took a six-foot whip on a fourteen-inch rolling stock. It had a twelve or fourteen inch "cracker" on the end of the tapered platted leather. This was made from what we called "seiggrass" string, a better name is binder twine. It was small strands that had been rolled together and then rolled with other strands to form a larger string. When the whip is used correctly, the cracker will sound as sharp and loud as a pistol shot. We were allowed to use the whips, but never to bring a serious injury to the animal.

The hunt had been successful. I had found the pig and he was on his way back to the pen. We were only fifty yards from the broken fence, when suddenly Mr. Boar decided he didn't really want to go back home. We were just off the gravel road in the weeds of another fence corner, when I decided to end this resistance and brought the whip into play. The first crack of the whip alarmed the boar, but it alarmed the horse the most. In the next few seconds, I was trying to calm Charlie down when Mr. Boar decided a charge was in order. With his head partly sideways (a hog must turn his head sideways to attack a standing object), he was coming at Charlie, who had some concern about his forelegs.

What did I do? Prayed a lot I am sure, but together we put immediate distance between us and the big boar hog. I dismounted and found a very big stick. Now this is a weapon that even a boar can understand. I tackled the job on foot and the boar gave way. With a few well-placed blows, Mr. Boar headed for that hole in the fence. Weren't you scared? Yes, to the point of shaking. Why didn't you just run away? Because Grandpa would not accept that kind of behavior. You run only to save your life and not before.

Grandpa probably expected too much, but then Dad did too. Both knew what it took to make a man. Grandpa feared neither man nor beast yet he was not boastful, and above all he was not careless around dangerous situations. The fight is long over, the fear subsided, and the fence is mended. I had learned a serious lesson. Don't try to drive an angry boar hog on horseback with only a whip, especially if you are riding a little bay horse named Charlie.

The Campaign Cigar

A Short Story by Dr. Harry E. Carr

Daddy was into politics. I admit that I didn't understand much about them, but I was quite proud of him as he ran for a county office. I remember that there were lots of meetings to attend. It was hard to elect a Democrat in Hardin County, and equally as tough to upset an incumbent that had been there for decades. But Dad was game for the office, and made several preparations to insure a victory. This included cigars to be handed out to the smokers. They were symbols of success, and I am sure Daddy wanted to appear a victor in this campaign even before it was started.

The cigars came in a beautiful wooden box. I remember it well because I wanted that box. What a wonderful place to store the treasures of a boy! Jake and I had a special shooting marble that we called a "toll", which deserved special treatment. I also had a few empty twenty-two shells that I had picked up at the local fair's shooting galley one year, which made good soldiers. Jake and I would split up

Then we would take turns sliding our washer across the floor to destroy the "enemy". Who ever had the most still standing won the game. After a few games, it was put away until another rainy day. Perhaps these items could be stored in that special box.

Maybe I would store a special coin that I had or something that had been given to me by some favorite person. But the box wasn't empty yet, I knew because I checked it often. The cigars were smaller than regular cigars, but much larger and longer than a cigarette.

I kept hoping I would find the box empty and then I could ask for it. Then one day it hit me, Jake and I could help out. I had never smoked a cigar. I had puffed a time or two on a cigarette, but nothing serious because the cigarette smoke made me strangle and cough.

Someone had said that a cigar was milder and sweeter than a cigarette. Of course, having nothing to gage the flavor or sweetness by, I believed them. The morning came for our great experiment. We had the matches and I took two cigars from the box. Now I knew the procedure, you bit off the end and spit it out before you smoked the cigar. Boy was that a big mistake! Some of that juice found its way down inside and I was already feeling sick.

The Smoke

It was a sunny morning, just perfect for our adventure. Mom and Grandma were busy in the kitchen, getting ready for the noon meal. The cigars were stored in Mom's chest of drawers. The chest had an arched top with two doors that opened outward. There were two shelves that were usually stacked with pillowcases and sheets; this was where the two wooden boxes of good cigars were stored.

Out Behind the House

We hid on the west side of the old farmhouse behind the large stone fireplace. The fireplace came all the way to the ground and protruded out from the house by at least two feet. The massive stones created, at least in our childish opinion, an excellent hiding place. I suppose we thought the smoke would travel up the chimney and disappear above the house.

Lighting Up

It was light up now or die; sorry that was wrong, it was light up and die. The glow of the big country match was touched to the end of two newly properly licked cigars. You see that's what adults did to keep the cigars from coming unwrapped. That was another big mistake, the tobacco juice was swallowed. I cannot think of anything the stomach reacts to as quickly as tobacco juice.

Two or three puffs and I was coughing, my eyes were watering and I felt like I was going to die. The tobacco juice was kicking like a mule in my stomach. Jake had fared no better. Two of the sickest boys you ever saw crawled upon the long front porch, and lay down together to die.

We were on the far end of the porch. It was closer to the ground, and a good place to put your head over the edge to vomit, and we did. Boy! Would a drink of water taste good, but I was too scared to go into the house. We figured that if the tobacco didn't kill us, Daddy surely would when he found out.

Discovery

Mom found us still lying on the end of the porch. Since death was so near, we were both glad to see her. Now it was always better to be found out by Mom than it was by Dad. She would do a lot of hollering but seldom was she more severe than that, and if she was, it was by a hickory from the old peach tree.

It took no detective to unravel this case. Smoking cigars lay in plain sight on the bare ground near the old fireplace chimney. They had had been hastily dropped by two very sick boys. Mom rebuked us in her sharpest tone, and gave a fine lecture against kids smoking. That was ever her way, when she was really upset she could wax quite elegant.

A Lecture Wasted in Time

At that time, her lecture, as fine as it might have been, wasn't needed. I was not sure of making it through the day, and I never wanted to see another cigar as long as I lived. What we needed now was water, barrels and barrels of it. Something had to give, but water only hit the bottom of my stomach and refused to stay. Up it came again. Was there no end? It was the same uneasiness for Jake.

Too Sick to Eat

Dinnertime came. The big dining table was my favorite place to be at this time of day, but for the life of me, I wanted absolutely nothing to eat. I just wanted to die in peace. It was one of the most miserable afternoons that ever I spent. I knew that I had to get better before I could die, for I was far too sick to die today.

The Cigar Box

Did the cigar box ever get empty? Yes it did, but by that time I had lost all interest in it. Why? Because when I opened it, the smell of cigars that lingered inside brought back bad memories of a day not so long ago. I wanted nothing to do with it, for it nearly cost me my life. Well, at least one miserable summer afternoon.

Daddy's Home

I sure dreaded Daddy coming home from the mine, I just knew that our troubles were not yet over. I saw the car coming up the driveway and made myself scarce. He didn't get into the house before Mom told him. You notice I said Mom, I was well around the corner of the house but still within earshot. The road was open before me, but I knew better than to run. But Daddy just laughed, he knew that no punishment in the world could be worse that what we had endured that afternoon. I agreed with him whole heartily.

Losses

Daddy lost the election, I lost the box, and Jake and I lost a summer day. However, we weren't doing much that day anyway. Out by the side of the house, hidden behind the fireplace, we had learned another valuable lesson of growing up - boys should not smoke cigars. It was quite dangerous, biting off the end of the cigar and running your tongue over the cigar before lighting up. I believe we also learned that smoking did not make a man out of a boy.

I think we also learned that the days of summer are far too short and far too busy to spend another day on the end of the old country porch wrapped up in self-inflicted agony.

The Lime Spreader

A Short Story by Dr. Harry E. Carr

Spring and A Pile of Lime

The farm was old, but new to us. It was located nine or ten miles from where we once lived. It even had a new postal address, but Grandpa would not be out done. A rural route from the former address of Elizabethtown ran a mile farther down the gravel road, and so our mailbox went up on the route out of Elizabethtown instead of coming from Golconda. It didn't make sense to me, since the route from Golconda ran much nearer. But then, that was the way it was. There was neither room for discussion nor argument.

This was as the last farm had been, a share cropper farm. And like most of those farms, it had suffered from neglect. There were plenty of bushes to be cut from the fields and sage grass to be burned from the "pasture" field. The bushes had to be "grubbed", that is to cut below the surface of the ground with axe or grubbing hoe. They had to be cut deep enough not to catch the plow point or cultivator shovel when they passed over them.

For the first time, we had to care for a herd of semi-tame cattle that belonged to the owner. These cattle were not use to coming to the barn nor were they that friendly with people. They wintered in the woods a quarter of a mile from the house, and were fed only when the grass had died and been picked down too low to graze on.

Both house and barn needed repair. There was a large fireplace in each of the two main bedrooms; however, Grandpa stopped up the one in their room and cut a hole in the wall so that he could insert a stovepipe into the chimney. Now he could have his wood stove in the living room, which was also their bedroom. The barn had not been cleaned in years, so spring came and there was much barn cleaning. I never much cared for this one, boards were loose, especially in the hayloft, and the doors needed repaired as well.

There was no building for the blacksmith's shop on this farm, so the shop was set up in the open space between the garden and the barn. The tools were packed in a huge box with a corrugated roofing nail securing the lid. The bellows and forge were firmly set, and the vise and manual drill press were mounted to a post set firmly in the ground, along with a corresponding workbench. The great anvil rested on a standing section of log that was cut just for that purpose.

Liming

It was a beautiful morning in early spring, when Grandpa and I left the barn. Today we would scatter the lime from a pile that had been dumped on the edge of the field last fall. Lime that has lain in an uncovered mound through the fall rains and winter snows tends to solidify. Interpreted, that means that before you shovel, you must break the heavy crust. I was glad my shovel was a dirt spade. Grandpa had a corn scoop and he loaded it full to the tip.

After we had a load on the wagon, seven or eight hundred pounds, we were ready to hitch onto the lime spreader. According to plans, Grandpa would drive and I would shovel lime into the spreader; however, there was another slight problem. The lime spreader, with its fan under the hopper, had set partly loaded with lime throughout the winter. Frankly, I didn't believe that the lime spreader would ever work again.

After breakfast, and it was always good at Grandma's there was homemade biscuits with bacon or pork shoulder and lots of white gravy, we harnessed out a team. Soon, the wagon was rolling through the barn lot gate. We were on our way to the lime pile. Grandpa didn't talk much except to himself, and that was in far too low tones for a boy to overhear; however, when we sat down to rest or at night, he always had a story to tell. I did not think that I would remember them, but they stuck in a young and impressive mind.

I was confident that he was the best horseman I knew and the best blacksmith in the county. He taught me a little about being a blacksmith. To this day, I never pick up a garden hoe to sharpen it without remembering him. He had a special way of sharpening it and I still sharpen it just as he taught me to do.

On the Way to the Field

It was a beautiful spring morning, the cloudless sky promised to be a warm spring day, and Grandpa was at the reins. He seldom surrendered the driving of the horses to anyone; however, occasionally he had me drive so that he could correct any flaws he observed, and did he ever observe! Grandpa was both a skilled driver and seemed to know how to get the best out of the team. I never saw one of his teams that wouldn't give him their best in a pull or in a spoken command. We always carried a six-foot whip with a fourteen-inch "seigrass cracker". You could crack it but you best never leave a mark on the horse or mule.

Grandpa was anxious to start this morning; it would be an all day job so we left the barnyard in a trot. It wasn't long until we had reached the lime pile; it was only a half-mile away. Soon we had a working hole broke through the crust and was loading the lime. It was hard work, but soon the pile would be gone. Once the wagon was loaded, Grandpa backed the horse up to the two-wheeled lime spreader and secured it to the wagon, but the team of horses could not budge the heavy spreader. The solidified lime had firmly locked both wheels. I could see Grandpa becoming angry, when he started to do something he meant to finish it.

Soon the lime spreader was unhitched and we were headed for the barn still carrying our load of lime. Grandpa did not explain what he was going to do. The set of his face made asking a question an unthinkable thing. A quick trip back to the barn and we were soon hitching another team to the front of the first team. Once another tongue was attached to the permanent tongue of the wagon, we had a four-horse hitch. This was not necessary new, we often worked a three-horse team on certain equipment, and on rare occasions, we would have two teams hitched to the same load. Pulling the hay baler was usually a four-horse hitch.

The lime spreader set where we had left it. We had come back to the field in a must faster trot, even with the load of lime. Again we hitched to the lime spreader, we had the horsepower now, at least we thought so. Again the horses could not budge the lime spreader; we dragged it a little but no wheels turned.

Two More Horses

Now grandpa was really angry. Unhitching from the lime spreader, we drove back to the barn and caught out two more animals. These were mules and they were placed in the short hitch next to the wagon. The wagon was now pulled by a six-horse hitch, I had never driven a six-horse hitch, but apparently Grandpa had. This time, we left the barn lot on the fly. A quarter mile down the gravel road we had to make a sharp left turn. I sat down flat in the wagon bed for this, because now the six-horse hitch was not just trotting, they were in a full gallop. I thought we would never, never, make the corner!

We made the corner! The wagon slid viciously to the right and then suddenly we were around the corner and the lime pile was in sight. There would certainly be no problem pulling that spreader now. I tried to tell Grandpa it was made for a tractor, but that did not make any difference to him. We would definitely pull it now!

With the lime spreader secured to the wagon, Grandpa gave the command and that lime spreader was moving but the wheels would not turn. We were leaving two long bare skid marks behind it. For although we could pull it, not one wheel turned and without the rotation of the wheels the fan that spread the lime would not turn. We dragged the spreader around and beat on it until either Grandpa or the horses were tired. Anger gave way to common sense, that spreader just would not work.

"You didn't spread any lime that day did you?" Well, I see you didn't know Grandpa very well. I sure wished that spreader had worked, because we spread lime all day by hand. Shovel by shovel we spread it in a sweeping motion. I sure did wish that spreader had cooperated, but before dark that pile of lime was on the field. It may not have been as evenly as it should have been, but it was on the field.

Grandpa did not say a word about our failure. It wasn't a failure to him, just a deviation from his original plans. And as usual, we never talked about that day again.

A Cushion To Dream On

A Short Story by Dr. Harry E. Carr

The Farmhouse

The living room in our farmhouse on the Griffith farm was small. Entrance was gained through a single front door. There was actually two doors, the other opened into Dad and Mom's room and was seldom, if ever, opened. Once inside their room, on your left was Grandpa and Grandma's bed. It was very old fashion, with a straw mattress that was changed in the fall and spring. It was very high to climb into. I don't remember being in that bed one time. You just didn't play on the bed. On the other side of the room was the bed of my two aunts. One was just out of her teens and the other was still a teenager.

The Wood Stove

A stove set in the center of the far wall. It was a wood stove, but occasionally we would have a lump of coal to lay on the wood. Wood and coal had to be carried in every day and ashes were to be carried out. In the morning it would glow cherry red, but no matter what, it always seemed to grow cold during the long winter nights.

The Two Tables

If you faced the stove standing between the two beds, on the left would be the radio stand with its small green-eyed radio on it. The radio was our only connection with the outside world. It was near one of the three windows in the living room. On the other side was an old-fashion table about thirty inches square on top. It rested on four wood legs that were about thirty inches tall. It always had a scarf of some kind on it. Sometimes a Bible or book rested on it, but usually it was for the living room kerosene lamp. The table always set by the second window. The third window was blocked by Grandpa and Grandma's bed, only the top of the window could be seen over the high straw mattress.

There were only two rockers in the living room. If you wanted another chair it had to be one from the kitchen table, or you could just set on the lower bed of my two aunts. There certainly were no chairs for boys and girls, they simply set on the floor or in a vacant chair, providing no adult wanted to sit there.

Airplanes In the Sky

Airplanes passing over our house was a rarity in those days. If one came over, it was usually a small plane bound for Harrisburg, which had a very small airport that accommodated private or small planes but to my knowledge, nothing commercial. Or perhaps it was going to one of the larger cities nearby.

In the war years, beginning in 1941, we would occasionally see a trainer flying in our area, but it was seldom enough to bring folks out on the front porch to listen and watch. Most of the planes that passed by were the double-winged open cockpit type. They were not very fast, but were very noisy and maneuverable.

My knowledge of airplanes was limited to what little I had read and what very few we had seen in the air over our farm or on a visit to the county seat. Of course, there was no airport anywhere nearby, so I had never actually seen one on the ground.

This was the spring of 1939 and I was all of seven years old, too small to go to the field, except on special occasions, but of course, I was big enough to help with the feeding in the morning and evening. The rest of the time, there was a large creek and all kinds of places to explore, including the largest barn in the county.

This morning, I had heard a plane flying low over the house and dashed outside to the front porch. However, the plane flying low was already over Whoopee Cat Mountain and out of sight when I reached the front porch. To say I was disappointed would be an understatement. I imagined that if I were a pilot, I would fly around just a little bit, especially if I was over a farmhouse so all could see me. Even I knew it was a foolish thought, but I thought it anyway.

Two Boys and A Summer Day

Summer days were too short to waste and there was so much to do. The spring that flow from under the old elm tree had a little branch that flowed northwest to enter the big creek down by the main water hole. Its little branch was bordered by some kind of mint plants that even in early spring gave off a fragrant odor. Frogs were busy establishing their territory and tuning their deepest masculine voice for the mating season. Birds were hopping about trying to catch an unwary worm or careless bug or perhaps even a sturdy stem to add to that new nest under preparation.

The little brook and the creeks offered many places to explore. There was another branch that circled in back of the house and ran nearly a quarter of a mile to that same big creek. We were surrounded by water although the creeks were not deep or big. Mother did not seem to worry about our boyish wanderings.

We were dressed in denim overalls (we always were) that were well worn and patched in more than one place, but they were always clean when we put them on. Of course, they didn't stay that way very long.

A Sling Shot

In my hip pocket, I carried the formable weapon of every farm boy I knew. It was a slingshot made with a forked tree branch about four inches in overall length. The Y shaped stick was perhaps five-eighths to three-quarters of an inch in diameter. On the top of each fork of the Y, a rubber band about a half inch wide and seven or eight inches long was fasted with string tightly wound about the rubber that was bent over the wood. The two rubber bands were slipped through two slits cut in the soft leather tongue of a discarded shoe, making a pocket to hold the projectile. The projectile was a smooth well-shaped rock.

This was a formable weapon in the hands of a country boy. A strict code was always in forced - you did not shoot at anything you did not wish to kill. Birds were off limits and so were any windows. I usually always had a few good rocks in my pocket. I searched every creek branch and along the road for the perfect rock. I had heard that David in the Bible had done this. Although our slingshots were vastly different, I too looked for just the right stones.

The Day Begins

This morning, we would walk along the spring branch and explore the creek beyond the water hole. I decided that I would go after the very potent projectiles at the blacksmith shop. It was down past the old elm tree just off the main road. Grandpa, when he fashioned horseshoes and turned the cork on the back of the shoe, usually had a little too much material and he would cut off little slugs. They made good projectiles.

"Why would you need the sling shot?" You don't need a reason! It didn't matter, you just carried it, and every boy I knew did. There were always snakes along that creek branch looking for those frogs just tuning up for spring. "Didn't you ever catch a snake when you were a boy?" Absolutely not! Never in my life did I catch or handle a snake. I started shooting when I saw one and kept shooting until I killed it or it escaped into the weeds. Besides Jake my little brother was with me, he always was, and today would be no different. I had to protect him. He couldn't run as fast as I could, so we'd have to stand and fight it out with any snakes we saw.

We left the front porch at the low south end and angled across the yard towards the coal pile in the northwest corner. We came to the main road, only a dirt road with a little gravel, which dead-ended at our barn, and now we were on our way to the blacksmith's shop.

A Great Find

There lying in the road, right under the old elm tree guarding the way to the shop, lay a beautiful white leather cushion. It was of the softest leather I had ever felt, in fact, I had never in my life seen anything like it. It was about four inches thick with two shiny hooks on the backside.

The cushion was about a foot and a half wide and maybe two and a half-foot long. But where did it come from? Elm trees do not produce cushions. I had never seen one as nice as this one. But where did it come from? That evening, I showed Dad my prize. He said that he believed it was the backrest from a seat of an open cockpit airplane. It was probably that one I had heard early in the morning. Dad said I could keep it, unless of course the owner of the plane came looking for it. I imagined that the pilot had done one of those upside down flips and it just fell, but I was so glad it landed near our old elm tree.

A Cushion to Dream On

The cushion became, for years to come, my proud personal possession. Of course I shared it with Jake, sometimes willingly and sometimes under duress. Jake remembers the cushion as gray, but that was the stain of the years and not the original color.

I set on it, sprawled on it, slept on it, but most of all I dreamed on it. It became a great place to sprawl out on and listen to the radio, if you didn't get stepped on. You could dream of places far away and adventures of a lifetime.

During the war years, war novels became quite popular. My favorite was about two aviators, one American and the other British. Dad would read the stories aloud while I dreamed on that cushion. I would be a pilot and fly to imaginary places all over the world to fight the enemy.

The cushion held the memories of childhood and growing up. The soft leather was such a pleasant place to live in my imagination and to make plans for the years of growing up. To wish and hope and certainly to be all you could be. As I grew older the cushion got less and less used, as I was busy taking my place in the field. Occasionally, I would find an hour or two to rest on its soft leather. Soon it was retired to a back support in a seat in our home, but locked inside those slightly stained leather covers were all the whispered dreams of a boy growing up. It was a gift from the sky, a loss to a pilot but a boon to a boy.

Leaving the Cushion Behind

When I married and moved away, I left the cushion at home. Somehow it seemed appropriate at the time. Unfortunately, Dad's house was destroyed by a fire and with it the cushion.

Remembering the Dreams

Sometimes I think of the old cushion and sentimentally I can hear again the mighty hoof beats of the great horse Silver and picture the masked hero riding to the rescue. Sometimes just after supper, the family gathered in the living room and there by the kerosene lamp, Dad read the stories of air battles in the skies over Europe.

When the war news was especially bad on the radios, and the hours seemed very dark for America, it was good as a family to be encouraged by the stories of brave men and daring deeds in the skies over Germany. (Even though, they were just fictional). Dad's voice was clear and he read with much emphasis, pausing here and there to let our imagination catch up.

While he read, I clung to my cushion and dreamed. I was one of those pilots streaking through the skies in my P-38 in hot pursuit of the enemy. Long after the lights were blown out and the only sound in the house was the crackling of the fire in the old wood stove, I could still fly my dreams.

I feel a bit sorry for children with no imagination, no dreams, and no great childhood memories, maybe it was because they had no cushion on which to sprawl and dream the dreams of growing up.

Candy, The Essence of Childhood

A Short Story by Dr. Harry E. Carr

When I was a little boy, candy around our house was scarcer than hen's teeth. You're right hen's teeth do not exist and neither did candy. There was only one time in the year that we could look forward to candy - during the Christmas season. Daddy usually brought it home on Christmas Eve. On Christmas morning, our stocking had hard candy, some chocolate drops, and a piece of fruit in it. The stocking hung behind the stove and the heat cause the candy to melt together and stick to the stocking. I wondered about the wisdom of Santa Claus, he was ruining good candy. Candy never came in great quantity, it was amazing if any survived until New Year's Day.

Candy came to our house in four different forms. There were hard candy pieces of various flavors - chocolate drops, peanut brittle, peppermint, and sometimes, but very rarely, I was able to get a small bag of my favorite, coconut bacon strips. They consisted of shredded coconut and sugar cooked and pressed together in a solid sheet about one quarter inch thick and about eight by ten inches in size, which fit nicely into a cardboard box. A nickel or dime's worth was several large pieces broken from the piece in the box and put in a little brown paper bag. What a treasure! I clutched it tightly in my hand; of course I would share with Jake. We always shared whether we really wanted to or not, our parents were funny about sharing.

Christmas also brought oranges and tangerines, which are my favorites. They came by the dozen, but then, there were a dozen of us and they did not last long. Apples too were bought, but they were not as expensive and there were always more of them. Even the small stores had citrus fruit on sale during this season of the year. If we went to Krogers in Rosiclare, they had a much larger selection and better fruit that was usually a bit cheaper and Daddy seemed to like that pretty well.

A One Room School

Bassett was the one room school located just over a mile from our old farmhouse if you walked around the road, and we always did. School was one of my favorite places to be.

When I was in school, I had paper and a pencil and could write. We had pencils at home but seldom any paper. To compensate, I would use grocery bags and cut them into small pages of uniform size. I punched holes into them, and bound them by lacing twine through the holes. These made little tablets, a kind of personal notebook that I could carry in my pocket. If possible, I always seem to have a pencil and a piece of paper on me. Years have passed, many changes have come but one thing has changed little, I always have something to write with and something to write on.

I liked books. Reading and writing I enjoyed; however, recitation was a bit difficult for a bashful boy. When it was time for recitation, whichever grade and whatever subject it was in, the entire class came forward and sat together on a recitation bench. The students took turns reading or solving arithmetic problems placed on the blackboard or answering history or geography questions.

I carried my books with pride, except when I started home and then one of the older girls that walked with us carried them. I was small for my age and everybody seem to try to help me out.

Christmas at the Local School

Christmas came to the local school with just as much anticipation as we had at home. The school always had a cedar tree for their Christmas tree. Cedars were plentiful in our area, while pines were as scarce as candy in the summer. Later the government bought up a lot of the old homesteads and seeded them with pines, but that was long after I was out of grade school. A local farmer usually supplied the tree.

Going After the Tree

The older boys chosen for the special honor of selecting the tree were dismissed at lunchtime, and with a saw or axe, they marched off to cut down that special tree. Usually one or more of the boys knew the best place to go; however, they always made an afternoon of it, returning just in time to get their books and go home for the day.

Tomorrow, we would nail two boards in a cross on the bottom of the tree. There was no such thing around our school as a tree stand; in fact, I did not even know such a thing existed. At home, we used the same type of stand on our Christmas tree, that is after we finally started having a tree.

Decorations Made With Love

Decorations were handmade. Construction paper wasn't always available, so we colored the paper taken from our school tablets. The paper was coarse and rough, but it took both colors and glue well. Soon great chains of red and green loops hung on the tree. A few pieces of roping sometimes survived proceeding years, but the strands were neither long nor were they bright anymore, but they did add character to our tree.

Sometimes the teacher would buy, at his or her own expense, a box of tinfoil icicles. In those days, there were no electric lights, because our school did not have electricity. We didn't have any glass ornaments either, but in our eyes, the tree was always beautiful.

The Drawing of Names

Each grade drew names to exchange gifts. The gifts could cost no more than five or ten cents and were wrapped in everything from newspaper to cheap Christmas paper. After the exchange of gifts, we sometimes had a short Christmas presentation, a play, some poems, or some readings. It was especially nice when the teacher read a Christmas story, and then when all was done, it was time to go home.

The teacher usually handed out a little treat bag to each student. It contained either an apple or an orange and one stick of candy for each student. Sorry to say, most students did not appreciate the sacrifice that the teacher made to buy those little goodies at Christmas. I may not have appreciated the sacrifice, but I sure enjoyed the candy.

A stick of candy was a stick of candy and it was still a few days until Christmas. I tried to make it last for a couple of days, which is a very difficult thing for any young boy to do.

A Store in the Hollar

When we went to visit Shawnee Hollar [Hollow], there was in years gone by, a little store near the forks of the road. It was made from rough lumber from the sawmill. A small board covered each joint in the boards.

The main road from Elizabethtown went past Keeling Hill School and the Keeling Hill General Baptist Church in the valley below. Beyond the church, the road passed by the home of Dr. Birch, the dentist. The home was a beautiful building set some fifty or so yards from the banks of "Hog Thief" creek.

There was no bridge; you must ford the creek to cross. It was shallow at this spot except when it rained. It was good to be on the side of the creek you wanted to be on when a "gully washing" rain came. The ford was a little longer than most, the distance was probably ten to fifteen yards. The bottom of the creek was brown creek gravel with only an occasional larger stone. The rocks were worn round and smooth from tumbling down the creek.

Daddy always drove a truck, and in the summertime our seat was a quilt spread out in the truck bed. It was highly unlikely that a truck would ever get stuck in the gravel; however, the occasional driver seemed to do it. Dad never stuck, not even once. Sometimes, I hoped he would get stuck, then we could get out in the water and push like the others did. Less than a quarter of a mile further, the road intersected with another road coming in from the Old Furnace. It was an old iron ore smelting furnace now long abandoned, with the top stones slowly slipping from their lofty perch and sliding down in a heap at the bottom.

The Old Furnace dated back to the Civil War era. The signs of its use could be found up and down the gravel road. You could find with little effort, fragments of slag that were bigger than a man's fist. The slag was wasted rock that had been crystallized by the extreme heat of the furnace. Each piece of slag looked and felt like black glass.

The Store On Hog Thief Creek

The store building was on the left side of the Old Furnace road. A porch ran the length of the front, and the posts were poles from the woods. What is rustic now, was cheap in those days. The owner may have lived in the back of the store, I don't quite remember. The store was about twenty feet wide and maybe forty feet long. It was not painted; the rough sawn lumber had taken on a weathered look of gray.

Here, at the intersection, you went to the right to go to Shawnee Hollar. The narrow road ran up the high creek banks of Hog Thief and then turned back into the bottoms.

Daddy sometimes stopped at the country store to buy a few things, and then continue on to the house of our relatives. The store seldom had any fresh vegetables, except those locally grown and only those in season. The shelves had a few cans of this and that, some dry goods, flour, meal, sugar, and salt. A few bars of the same brand of hand or laundry soap. The laundry bars smelled a little like homemade lye soap and were used both for dishes and laundry.

There were no washing powders. Clothes were washed using a wash board. A wash board was a frame with two legs and a brass metal covering with ridges, one following another. Clothes were washed by dipping them in the hot water of the tub, rubbing them with soap, and pushing them up and down on the wash board until they were clean. The water was rung out by hand. Few had hand operated wringers, and no one, to my knowledge, had such a device in the hollar.

A few pair of overalls and shirts were stacked on the counter on the left with a few bolts of cloth for making clothes. The left side of the store, just after you entered, was my favorite place. There was a small candy counter that was never full, but did have a box or two of candy, some candy sticks standing in a glass container, and the ever present bubble gum.

A small pop container filled with ice from the icehouse out back contained several bottles of pop. They were five cents a bottle, except the small bottles of coke that were a dime. Only a few would pay a dime for eight ounces of pop when you could get twelve for a nickel. Sometimes, but rarely, Dad would buy a pop for us to share. I don't think parents thought much about passing on germs in those days. We took turns drinking until the bottle was empty. Two or three pennies or sometimes as much as a nickel would be shared together at the candy counter.

For a penny, you could get two pieces of gum, a small bag of candy, which usually consisted of a few pieces of coconut bacon strips and three or four chocolate drops, and maybe there would be enough to have a stick of one of the striped candies. Sometimes they would have horehound or liquorice candies, but I did not care much for either. Horehound candy tasted a lot like medicine and liquorice tasted like tobacco.

Jackson's on the Hill

Jackson's store was located at the crown of Courthouse Hill in Elizabethtown, the county seat. It was a two-story building with a long flight of stairs running up the side of the courthouse with offices located on the second floor. There was a parking lot between the store and the courthouse, and just behind the courthouse almost in a straight line with Jackson's store, was the red brick jailhouse.

The Smells

Jackson's store always had the mixed smell of fresh ground coffee, pickles, and bananas as most stores did in those days. The smell, which was the strongest, depended on where you were standing in the store.

A stalk of bananas hung from the ceiling. When you bought bananas, they were cut from the stalk with a hook bill carpet knife. The stalk would hang there until it was empty. Grandpa would try to get the empty stalks. Why? He hung them in the chicken house, believing they would control chicken mites. Did they? I don't think so, but it didn't matter what I thought, as long as Grandpa thought it would work it would hang wherever he said.

There were dry goods galore; at least it seemed that way to me. A small barrel contained pickles floating in brine and another held dry white soda crackers. White Great Northern beans from Michigan filled a large bin behind the counter. The beans had arrived by grocery truck in large burlap bags lined with some type of paper. From the bin, they were dipped with a large scoop, placed in a bag, and weighed.

You did not buy beans by the pound, but by stating the amount of money you wanted to spend. We either ordered a quarter or fifty-cent bag depending on available money, which was a very sizeable bag of beans.

Run Up to Jackson's Store

When we worked the gristmill, often we were often sent to Jackson's store for tobacco, they handled the brand our parents used. Jake and I always liked it when we were sent to Jackson's. Mr. Jackson, a jovial older man, would go to the candy counter and take out two pieces of candy and give one to each of us. Sometimes he would take out four pieces of candy and give us two each, one to eat now and one to put in our front pocket for tomorrow. What a great way to impress two little boys in those days of yesteryear.

Pleasant Memories

The old store on the hill still holds pleasant memories; the smells come back, and in my mind I can located every item in the shop. But the best of memories was of a jovial shopkeeper that opened the door of his candy counter and found candy for little boys who had no money. His thoughtfulness and kindness left sweet memories of the days of summer, and of a little tow-headed boy always broke but with an insatiable craving for candy, almost any variety or kind but preferably in large quantities.

Riding Old White Face

A Short Story by Dr. Harry E. Carr

Riding A Cow to the Barn

She was a brindled cow with a white face that we called old white face, if she had a name beyond that, I have forgotten. She was part of the milking herd on the old Griffith farm. We never sold milk or cream in those days, we basically used all the milk and butterfat. We drank a lot of milk that had been cooled in the spring flowing from under the old elm tree down by the blacksmith shop, or that had been suspended in a sealed bucket hung by a rope into the well to cool for supper. Fresh butter from the old brown churn was always on the table. It covered many a piece of fresh cornbread, biscuit or a fresh ear of corn.

After the morning milking time, the cows were driven a quarter of a mile to the back pasture. The pasture was a beautiful hillside rolling away towards a little spring branch that ambled its way through its entire length. At the farthest end was a wood lot, where on a hot day, the cows could find shade from the sun and lay down to rest and chew their cud, while swishing pesky flies.

The dusty path, which led to the north pasture, was comfortable to walk barefooted. The dust was fine as face powder and swished up between your bare toes as you walked. The path ran along the west fence row wobbling in and out whenever there was a bush or some obstruction and then turned back again near the wire. The fence had a woven wire bottom and two strands of barbed wire on the top. It was one of those fences referred to as "horse high and pig strong." It wasn't a long walk but one you had better pay attention to, because sometimes the cows left unexpected deposits in the path that could make a mess out of your bare feet.

Better to Ride than Walk

There was an alternative to walking. If a lazy way can be found to do anything you can depend on a boy to find it. My two uncles had broken Old White Face to ride. They were just eight years older than I was. I noticed they never walked back to the barn, they always rode on the white-faced cow. They were much bigger than I was and getting astride the cow was much easier for them. It wasn't a long ride and the cow didn't seem to mind once you were aboard.

All Aboard - If You Can Get Aboard

Getting on White Face's back was my biggest problem. At eight years old I was far too small to just jump on her back. When all the other cows headed for the barn so did she, and she was not about to wait for a barefoot boy to get on her back. Once astride Old White Face, she gave me no problem and I could jump off just as she reached the great hallway of the barn. One did not want to stay on her back until she was in the stall, for just over the door someone had foolishly nailed a one by six board that could surely strip you from a cow's back.

Rigging the Gate

I came up with a plan. It was a perfect plan in the mind of a young boy, but then I thought all my plans were good. The gate to the pasture was three strands of barbed wire fasten solid to the gatepost on the north side. There was a center post that held the strands in place and another small post at the south side. The gate was opened and closed by inserting the free small post into a wire loop at the bottom of the gatepost and slipping another wire loop over the top of the small gatepost.

It would have been easier had there been a regular gate. I could have just partially closed the gate and forced the cows to come near the great post on the south side of the gate. However, a wire gate does not lend itself to that particular thing. I kept trying to rig a way to hold the limp gate into the proper position so that only one cow could come through at a time. If this worked, then when Old White Face came through she would be near enough, at least I hoped, for me to jump on. Now there are many things to consider in this project. First, if I missed and fell under her feet, she was going to step on my bare feet. Secondly, if I jumped too hard and fell on my stomach, it would likely knock the wind out of me and I would fall off anyway. But life always has its hazards, and one must be willing to take an occasional risk if only to ride to the barn.

A Leap of Faith

Here she comes! I bunched every muscle in my body for the jump, but old White Face knew and she always hugged the far side making my jump as far as possible. But close or far,

I must jump. This time I knew I would succeed. Sometimes I did, but there were other times when I just slid down her side to the ground. I believe that Old White Face cow was the only cow in history that had fingernail marks down her left side. I didn't make it again, but I dug in to make the fall less painful.

Give Up? Never!

When will you give up? I don't think that I ever gave up as long as we owned Old White Face. She was the challenge of going after the cows, and I don't remember one time when I didn't try to jump on her back. More often than not, I missed. It was indeed a rare occasion when I came to the barn riding on her back. Almost every day, I would try to figure out another way to get her close enough to jump onto, and every day she seemed to find a way to get farther away. I think I might have been as much a challenge to her as she was to me.

Summer's End

The green of the wood lot gave way to the brilliant hues of gold and brown. The green grass of the pasture was quickly turning its own shade of brown. Soon the cattle would spend more time in the barn lot munching hay. Before summer ended, I would ride Old White Face one more time. And so by a barbed wire gate propped up, I would make the last jump of another summer of my life. Next year, I would be bigger and surely I would ride every day! There would be a next year for me, but that winter Old White Face was sold. Next year there would be barefoot tracks in the paths of summer, but the triumphant ride to the barn would only be one of the memories of the summers of growing up.

There is a Snake in the Hen House

A Short Story by Dr. Harry E. Carr

Copperhead Snakes

Growing up in the south meant that snakes were common things. The copperheads were of the poison variety. They got their name from the copper color of their heads, which were the color of autumn's fallen leaves. Whether in the woods or under the shade tree, they blended perfectly with the copper leaves of the trees. They would strike without warning if you got too close or if they felt pressured. You could find them almost anywhere, in the woods, the fields, along the creek banks, or in the rocks.

Rattlesnakes

Then there was the rattlesnake. Their rattle was enough to scare most into a panic, and they had the same habitat as the copperheads. They gave a warning when you were too close to suit them; however, you were often too close before you were aware of it. The rattlesnakes seemed to like the rocks, bluffs, and caves much more than the copperheads. You could find one sunning on a bright morning or later in the day, laying in the shade of a rock or in a cave's cool confine. They were probably more poisonous than the copperhead, but they were not near as plentiful in our area.

Cottonmouths

There was also the water vipers, known as the cottonmouth. Their bodies were as black as indigo, but the inside of their mouth was as white as cotton, hence their name cottonmouth. These snakes would get quite large in girth; but were never much longer than four feet. They enjoyed curling up on a fishing pole that had been left in the water, or lying on a dark tree root, which they blended with perfectly. Of all the snakes in our community, I believed this to be the most poisonous.

The Non-Poisonous Variety of Snakes

There were house and garden snakes of all varieties. Most served a useful purpose I am sure; however, snakes and I did not get along. Sometimes a black snake, these snakes could get up to six feet long but were not very large in diameter, would get in the barn. They especially like it in the big corncrib. Grandpa would say, "Don't kill the snake in the corncrib, it will catch the mice and rats." But I followed the philosophy – "A man has got to do what a man has got to do." To me, no barn was large enough for any specie of snakes, regardless of the size. Trying to reach for a feed bucket by lantern light and touching the cold body of a snake coiled up in its warmth, is an exhilarating experience that I hope never to repeat.

Chicken snakes were as bad as black snakes. They were always looking for young chickens, goslings, baby turkeys, or eggs of any kind. One could often find a chicken snake around the hen house in the springtime of the year.

New Baby Chickens on the Farm

Every year Granny would order chickens from one of the hatcheries out of Harrisburg, Eldorado, or Equality. The chickens would be shipped through the mail. It was quite an experience to go into the local post office when several hundred of the chickens had arrived and were waiting to go out on the postal routes. The boxes of one hundred were divided into four compartments of twenty-five each. The bottom of the cardboard boxes was covered with excelsior, small round holes were in the sides, and the top was bound on with strapping or string.

Granny would have us watching the mailbox for the arrival of the baby chickens. It was surprising how many actually survived the trip; the hatchery usually added a few extras just in case some died.

The Brooder House

There was no electric lamp bulb that could be hung to give warmth to the new baby chickens. Lanterns were set among them or hung over them to provide some additional heat. Again some baby chickens would not survive, but most did.

The brooder house was an old building probably fifteen or twenty feet wide. The rough-sawed two by four rafters were sloped from the front to the rear of the building. They were sloped to run the water to the back of the building. The building was roofed with sheets of ribbed galvanized roofing. Once bright, it was now only a rusty brown.

The building had no windows and only one homemade door in the front. Of course, there were cracks in the building and holes under the edge of the roof.

Trouble in the Brood House

It was the spring of the year, supper was over and darkness came early. A heavy spring cloud made the darkness seem like pitch black. Down at the pond, the frogs were croaking with their best voices, inviting any interested girl frogs to join him. Suddenly, the night came alive with the sound of trouble in the brooder house. Grandma said, "There is something in the brood house, listen to those chickens." Even small chickens have a way of letting you know when they are disturbed.

The chickens were no longer just baby chicks; they weighed nearly a half-pound now. You had to keep an eye out for all types of predators, raccoons, skunks, large rats, and of course snakes.

Checking Out the Brooder House

By lantern light, we rushed out to the brooder house. Someone had brought an iron poker just in case it was a big varmint. I don't know who had it, but I think it was Grandma. You couldn't see very well by lantern light, but there were no animals moving around except the chickens. However, they were still in a state of chaos. We had been looking in the wrong direction. There he was up in the rafters, a long ugly chicken snake that was glaring down at us. How he got up there after eating two or three small chickens I never knew, all I could see was that ugly head peering over the small rafters.

Panic ensued, not only with the chickens but with us as well. I certainly did not want to stand under a loaded snake, and this one was loaded with chickens. Granny was determined that that snake nor any other snake that might be in the brooder house, was not going to have any more of her chickens. She was ready to rescue those he had swallowed, but of course they were already dead.

Making Battle Plans

The problem - how do you extricate a snake entwined in the rafters of a small building by lantern light. Suggestions flew around the brooder house, none I am afraid that were very practical. Someone suggested that we cut off the snake's head and squeeze the chickens out of him. Another, and it may have been me, suggested that we get Grandpa's bull shooting shotgun and blow his head off. However, in close quarters that was not only dangerous, but it would leave a gaping hole in the roof of the building.

But how in the world do you extract a snake full of chickens from a full brooder house? The snake was full and comfortable, and when he was hungry again there was plenty of food running around on the floor just below him. There he was, a full-grown chicken snake some five or so feet long with huge lumps inside that were of course undigested chickens.

A New Idea, Tongs from the Shop

Someone came up with the idea of taking the tongs from the blacksmith's forge, catching him by the head and dragging him outside so he could be properly dispatched without harm to the chicks. They were still running helter-skelter and we weren't helping matters very much. Now I did not volunteer to catch or pull that snake out. I was too short and if I were to pull the snake down, I would have to stand right under him. There was no way that I wanted a snake around my neck, whether he was full or empty. You see, I still opted for the much safer shotgun method. I thought it was logical, and it put me at a safe distance from that snake.

Handy Multipurpose Tools

It pays to have blacksmith tools around the house. One of the older boys ran out and brought back a big pair of black tongs, but those handles still seemed far too short to me. So, I gave them plenty of room to capture the snake. I am afraid that even my lantern holding was not too good. I was not about to get under that snake. Some argued that he was a non-poisonous snake, but such a snake did not exist in my thinking. They were all bad and all dangerous, at least to me.

The person handling the tongs captured the snake behind the head and the struggle began. You see, the snake had a pretty good hold on those rafters and so, with much pulling, the head came down and the body followed. The snake hit the floor pretty hard and the chickens scattered again, but this time the fellow with the tongs was in control. The snake was dragged outside and someone quickly dispatched it with a sharp axe from the wood yard. The ingested chickens were beyond any rescue or recovery.

Slowly, order came back to the brooder house. One of the lanterns was left in the brooder house and the chicks huddled around it, probably not out of fear but for the warmth. We searched both the inside and the outside of the brooder house, I might say it was done cautiously lest we find a mate for the snake, but we found nothing.

Night Feeding

I confess that after the events of that night I lost all desire to check on the chickens at night. During the day, I would fill the half gallon fruit jars with water and seat them on the little self-dispensing bowls and make sure there was feed in the feeding troughs.

It would be a long time before I could forget those little beady eyes staring down from the rafters. I never again entered that brooder house without first glancing upward, just in case.

The Catfish

A Short Story by Dr. Harry E. Carr

A Fishing Hole

The spring branch running from under the great elm tree meandered along through the peppermint plants to the creek just beyond. The creek had a ford there, which served as a waterhole for the horses and mules when they came in from work. It was indeed a small creek but to a small boy, it looked much larger than it really was. Mother spent a great deal of time trying to keep us boys away from that creek. She was deathly afraid of any water that was more than a few inches deep. However, any spring branch or creek has an irresistible appeal to an eight-year-old boy.

In the spring branches, on any hot summer day, you could build dams, paddle wheels, and float all types of little boats. It was a clean and cool place to spend the day, but for serious fishing one must go to where the fish were and there were a few in the big creek.

A few feet up the creek from the watering hole was a fishing hole. We might have caught a few small perch from it, but I was sure that greater fish were just lying on the bottom waiting for my hook and line.

Everybody Has A Fish Hook

What might have been true for some certainly wasn't true with us. It was another one of those dangerous items on mother's agenda that was to be kept away from small boys. Today, Jake and I would go after the big one, but all our searching yielded no fishhook. So we switched to an alternative. Grandpa had hog rings that looked just like a fishhook. The hog rings were put into a device that was shaped like a pair of pliers, and were pushed through the skin and flesh of a pig's nose to keep them from rooting up the pigpen. The hook was sharp but did not have a fish-retaining barb. Nevertheless, we were sure it would work, and so with a length of string and our knife to cut a short willow pole we headed for the fishing hole. The hook was so heavy it did not need a sinker.

A Serious Bait Problem

It wasn't that we couldn't find earth worms, they were plentiful enough, just lift up a board that had spent the summer on the ground and they would be squiggling underneath. But you must lift up that board cautiously, because underneath there could be a salamander, a small snake, a lizard, or some other type of dreadful creature.

With a Prince Alberta tobacco tin of worms we headed for the creek. Crossing at the ford, we moved up through the willows, well out of sight of the house and mother's watchful eye. I selected a fine willow fishing pole, about five or six feet long, and proceeded to cut it down. We called the length of strong string "stagin". It was a type of woven twisted string. Those were the days long before the nylon fishing line. It was tied securely at the top of the pole and to the edge of that bright copper hog ring.

A Small Worm and A Large Hook

A new problem presented itself. How do you get a worm on a hook that is as large as the worm itself? The hog ring was far bigger than a fishhook, and although it had a sharp point, it would take a lot of ingenuity to bait that hook. We were sure that if the catfish living down below saw any part of that gleaming hook he would simply move away. Sometimes on a bright day when the water was clear, you could see a few of the fish moving around in the fishing hole and especially this big catfish. I don't know why but they sure appeared to be a lot larger when they were swimming around in the bottom than they actually were when they were caught.

Digging through the slimy worms, I chose the largest one I could and dedicated him to that hook. After many desperate attempts the hog ring had a new coat of earthworm. You had to spit on the worm to make it work. I don't know why that was just the way it was. So with my best effort I spit on the worm, and just to ensure more good luck, Jake spit on the worm too.

A Poor Man's Float

We made a float by tying a piece of dead wood on the string. The line was tied in the middle of the stick; this would let us know if we had a bite. We had hoped that the dead float would keep the hook just above the bottom. No such luck, the hook was too heavy and the float was too small. Slowly it sank and lay in the mud on the bottom of the creek.

The Catch

For an eternity it seemed as though nothing happened. Only the rustling of the willow leaves by the slightest hot summer breeze broke the silence of the moment. Should we move the bait? Maybe we should try farther down the creek?

Suddenly the pole moved with a firm tug and with a mighty jerk the fish was flying through the air over our heads and out into the field beyond. We had done it; we had caught the catfish. That catfish was hardly big enough to keep, but keep him we did. Any fish that difficult to catch deserves to be eaten, especially by two little boys.

The Kitchen Table

A Short Story by Dr. Harry E. Carr

The Kitchen

The kitchen, with its old wood cook stove and its huge table, was one of the most important places in the house. The wood stove did not have a back with warmers and porcelain doors at the top, as many kitchen stoves had in those days. Out of the back of the stove came a six inch stove pipe, which went up one joint and a half then entered an elbow and went another two joints into the flu. The stove had four caps on top that could be removed, exposing the wood burning within. A large water reservoir went across the back of the stove, but I cannot ever remember water being in it. Hot water came from a big teakettle that was always on the stove. We never called the stove a kitchen stove; it was just the cook stove. A small ash pit formed a little porch in the front of the stove. It had a draft door with small slits that would light up the front of the stove on dark winter nights.

From this stove came all kinds of food, mostly fried or boiled. The only baked foods outside of breads were bread pudding, baked beans, or some kind of dressing, and occasionally a baked sweet potato with its "jacket" on. It was not only a treat for a meal, but it would fit nicely into a boy's pocket to eat later. Leftover cornbread could also be carried to the garden in the summer time, and green onions or a ripe tomato with corn bread was a snack that any boy of that day would have considered a treat.

I always searched the cornbread pan in the mornings; granny usually hid a small piece in the oven or somewhere else. Sometimes she would stuff it in one of my pockets with a sweet smile and a pat on the backside. Baked beans from the oven were one of my favorites. Leftover beans were drained, covered with black pepper, and baked until they were dry and then you could slice them like cornbread. On a winter evening baked beans with cornbread, buttermilk and fried potatoes made a great meal.

Another favorite from the oven was pork loins. I always thought granny baked them just for me. Now, I believe she baked them for everyone, but I'm pretty sure she had me in mind. Pork loins were fried right after hog killing time. They were packed in lard and sealed in a jar. Once opened and drained, they were put in between layers of dressing and then baked. Desert was usually some sort of fruit, but sometimes there was a bread pudding made with leftover biscuits and vanilla pudding that had been made from scratch.

Occasionally granny, because she was a deacon's wife, baked "preachers" bread. It was a mixture of flour, water, and shortening baked into cracker like portions to be used in the communion service. I would pester the fire out of granny until she would lay a strip or two on top of the stove and let it bake for me. It was the closest thing that we had to crackers. I would try to get as many strips as I could, but if you kept them until later, they became so hard that you had to soak them for a little while before you could chew them.

The big table must have been four foot wide and seven or eight foot long. Dad's family set on the bench along one side, and each had their place. Mom always held the baby so she could feed it from the table. There was no baby food or anything special; they just ate the soft food from the table. Grandpa set in the middle of the table on the other side and Granny sat next to him near the stove so she could wait on the table.

THE KITCHEN TABLE

It was always a big Saturday when we were able to buy a new "oil cloth" for the table. The oilcloth offered a new and tantalizing smell. I cannot describe the oil smell, but it filled the kitchen with an invitation to eat. The oilcloth was always bright and shiny with many colors; it graced the table well. Granny was always so proud of an oilcloth and urged great caution to be observed by all using it. She knew it would be many weeks or months before there would be another "oil cloth" bought. Granny and Mom made every effort to keep the table attractive and useful.

There was something about the table that still touches my heart when I think about it. Grandma never owned a matching set of dinnerware. In fact, if two or three pieces agreed in color it was a miracle. The dishes were bought a few pieces at a time from a farm auction or were a gift from someone who no longer wanted or needed that bowl, plate, cup, or saucer.

Setting the table just wasn't one of those things that were important to grandpa. As long as everyone had a plate, cup, or glass, and there were bowls for the food that was all that was important. He set no store in plates that matched or bowls that looked like they belonged on the table with the plates. He came to the table to eat not to admire the dishes.

Knifes, forks, and spoons were also of the assorted kind. One particular knife was always beside Grandpa's plate. It was a Case kitchen knife with wooden handles and a long thin limber blade. Grandpa used that knife in lieu of a fork with both deftness and skill.

Then again, most of the places I ate at as a boy did not have much better. I do not know why it bothered me, but I think it was because it bothered grandma. She didn't say it and she didn't ask for a set of dishes, at least not in my hearing, nor did she fuss about what she had, but I think I saw how important these things were during the early war years.

Oat flakes were popular and we had a few once in a while, but if you bought them, you best buy one brand, Crystal Wedding Oats. Why? In each box was a little glass bowl, a sparkling dessert dish. Granny collected each one with special care, and stacked them away in the cabinet. She was proud of her collection, never missing an opportunity to collect another.

THE KITCHEN TABLE

After my wife and I were married, we would sometimes go to see them at night, and it was never too late to cook. Granny would take her butcher knife and head for the smokehouse. With a lamp in hand, she would cut a ham or shoulder and fire up the cook stove. Soon, biscuits would be in the oven, ham or shoulder slices would be frying in the skillet and coffee and tea would be brewing on the stove. Her best dishes, none which matched, would grace the big table with its oil cloth covering. There were biscuits, ham and gravy, and jelly or sorghum molasses. Grandpa would bow his head and pray, "O Lord, we thank you…" and the rest of his prayer was lost in his mustache until he said amen. What memories rich and sweet flood my soul when I think again of these times!

I sometimes wish that I could go back and set Grandma's table with the best of china. But now that will not be necessary, for one day she will preside at a better table in a mansion somewhere in the New Jerusalem. All the dishes will match and she won't have to cook, but secretly I hope she will. I believe there will be a full table in her mansion, every dish will match, and there will be desert bowls at every place.

The Big Red Airplane

A Short Story by Dr. Harry E. Carr

I believe this event occurred the year after or maybe the same year in which I had found the airplane cushion. While I cannot remember the exact year, I certainly can remember the event well. We did not make long trips to the big towns in those days. On Saturday, a short trip into Elizabethtown provided us with everything we needed.

Daddy ran a gristmill in town that ground cornmeal that was used to make cornbread, cracked corn to feed the chickens, and a mixed dairy feed. Dad ground the corn cob and all. He also ground hay, alfalfa, clover, and other grains that were available. After they were ground very fine, he mixed them together. Dad also had a barrel of black strap molasses that had come up the river from New Orleans. They smelt good enough to eat, but I never tasted them. They just looked too black.

Occasionally, someone would come in and ask for thirty-two or sixty-four pounds of cracked corn; Daddy told me that he believed it was for a moonshine still. I didn't know what a still was or how it worked, and I certainly didn't know why they needed a certain weight of cracked corn.

In the 1940's when Dad got a better job working in the fluorspar mine, we occasionally went to the picture show in Rosiclare. It was only a short distance from Elizabethtown, perhaps four miles or more. In Rosiclare, you could see the water tower located along the Ohio River or the gazebo of the Rose Hotel located on a bluff overlooking the river. Rosiclare had only one main street with most of the stores located on its front, including the bank and theatre. In those days there was no floodwall, and when the Ohio got out of it's bank in the flood stage it always flooded the streets, sometime getting into the stores and theatre. The main street made a loop on the riverbank and turned back. There were side streets on which a few businesses operated, but mostly there were only houses.

I liked going to Rosiclare because they had a Kroger store there and sometimes we had money to buy fresh fruit, celery, and coffee that was ground in the store. Although I didn't drink coffee, it sure gave a pleasant aroma in the bag along with the celery and fresh fruit.

A movie was a dime and popcorn was a nickel, yet it must have seemed expensive when all of us went. There was always a double feature and we stayed and got our money's worth.

Profit Ventures to the Zoo

In later years, Dad would once a year or once every two years put a homemade cap on the bed of his pickup, add benches, and take a truck load of paying passengers to the zoo in St. Louis. It was an all day trip. The passengers brought along their lunches or did without, because few bought refreshments in the zoo due to high prices. In the late afternoon, everybody was rounded up and we would begin the long trip home. I remember going only once or twice during my childhood. When we went, we made every attempt to by-pass as much of the city as possible to avoid traffic and getting lost in such a big city.

Travel Was Slow

There were two or three cities within fifty to seventy-five miles that had a population of about eight to ten thousand; these seemed exceedingly large to a farm boy. A trip there once or twice a year was considered a trip of great length. It would take nearly an hour to drive the distance to Harrisburg, just a little over thirty miles away. Thirty-five or forty miles an hour was fast for the old cars in those days.

A Special Event

I never knew how Daddy found out about the event. Was there a billboard in town or an article on the radio? I don't know, there might well have been. I didn't care much for announcements or news, only the stories and the music of the Grand Ole Opera from Nashville or from our own Harrisburg station.

Two different hatcheries had radio programs. I remember one that came on with a guy playing a guitar and singing "Carter's chickery is on the air." You could order baby chickens, baby turkeys, baby geese, or baby ducks from the hatchery. Even guineas could sometimes be ordered. The guineas was a strange looking animal, with a head painted like a savage, dark bluish feathers, and the silliest voice you ever heard. Grandpa wouldn't allow them on the farm. He said they made too much noise, and it was true they were forever sounding, and loudly too!

You would be notified by mail of the prospective delivery date of your chicks. They didn't always come on that date, so you had to keep a close watch. When you came into the post office during chick season, both the chirping of the baby birds and the smell let you know that the back was full of baby chickens.

An Exciting Notice

There was a notice that a large airplane would be in Harrisburg and you could buy a ticket for a short ride, which would last about thirty or forty minutes. Daddy liked airplanes as much as I, and neither of us had ever flown. He wanted to go and take the family. There were only five of us at that time - Dad, Mom, Jake, myself, and Sis who was just a baby.

A Trip to Remember

It took more than an hour to get there. The airport, such as it was, had some type of hanger but there was no control tower or other amenities. A big brilliant red airplane set on the ground near one of the grass runways. The tail rested on a small wheel in the back, and the whole plane sloped backward. A crowd had gathered admiring the plane or trying to decide if they would take one of the flights. I think they wanted to see someone else ride first, and if the plane made the trip and landed again, they just might decide to fly too.

Mom and Flying

Mother never liked planes or flying, so she automatically elected to stay on the ground with Jake and Helen. I don't think she very optimistic about Dad and I flying, it seemed far too dangerous to her. As far as I know, mother only made one or two trips by air, and she would never board any plane without Dad. After Dad was gone, mother would not fly regardless of the occasion.

The Ride of A Lifetime

The big red plane was setting at the end of the take-off strip. It seemed like a long country lane to me. The side door of the plane was open and the steps were down for boarding. I could see the pilot and marveled that he could fly such a big plane.

When we were going up the steps, I clung tightly to Daddy's hand, he knew where he was going and I did not. I don't know how many passengers the plane seated, but I remember that there were two seats on either side and Daddy found one next to a window. I was seated comfortably on his lap waiting for something to happen. Strange, but these seat cushions looked very similar to the one I had found last year under the big elm tree down by the spring and the blacksmith shop.

In the Air

At last everyone for this trip was on board! The door was shut; it was too late for anyone to back out now. The huge motors begin to roar and the plane shook with every turn. Soon the plane began to move down the strip, I was traveling faster than I had ever traveled before, trees and poles were whizzing by. The front of the plane was now airborne and it was climbing up into the air.

Soon the plane was circling over one of the cities. I don't know which one that didn't seem important at the time. The houses looked so small, in fact, the entire city looked much like a toy village. I was really impressed to see the cars and trucks moving down the highway, I remember asking Daddy if they were real or just small cars. We flew over forests, streams, fields, and even a farmhouse in the distance. I remember wondering if they came out on their porches to see us go by. I felt very special flying today.

On the Ground Again

All too soon the ride was over and the airplane made it's decent to the airport. The ground was coming up too fast to suit me. I was so relieved when the wheels touched the ground and we were coming to a stop with the motors roaring.

The little door opened, the steps were let down, and we were soon leaving the plane. Mother seemed really glad to see us, I think she had been more scared than I. I had forgotten to be scared while we were flying. Somehow, I felt really special that day. I would never forget the day I flew with Daddy.

A Bright New Copper Penny

A Short Story by Dr. Harry E. Carr

A Rail Fence in November

It all happened one day in November, when I was seven years old. We were working on a rail fence at the end of the meadow that was on the southeast side of the barn. Grandpa and some of the boys were there and I was just watching. I was not near big enough to handle one of the fence rails.

A rail fence was a friendly fence to everyone. There were no barbs to dodge, and it was far easier to climb that a woven wire fence. This was the only rail fence that we had on the whole farm, except a few rails used to shore up the fence around the hog pen.

The Owner of the Farm

I had never met the owner of the farm, but I was sure that he must have been a very tough individual. He had mallard duck decoys stored in the barn loft and we had been severely warned not to touch them. I had the strongest suspicion that he would know that I had broken the taboo and had actually touched those mallard decoys on more than one occasion, and if he did know that it would be the end of me. If he didn't get me, Grandpa certainly would.

A Rabbit Hunt Long Ago

I saw his dogs long before I saw him, they were moving noiselessly through the grass looking for quails. We did not hunt birds; in fact, back then hunting was very rarely done by anyone in the family. The only hunt of any kind that I had ever been on was a rabbit hunt. I was four or five years old, and much too small to look over the high grass or briars.

While the dogs were running, Daddy stood me on a stump to watch. We were fortunate, the rabbit ran by us and Daddy shot him with his pistol, a 32-20 caliber. We had game, and that was all that was important. That was it. I never remember a hunt of any kind as long as we lived on the Griffith place.

Bird Hunter

I saw Mr. Griffith. He was coming around the hill from the distant wooded area and he was carrying a gun. Of course, why wouldn't he be carrying a gun? He was hunting and these were bird dogs. Grandpa and grandma had a fear of bird dogs; sometimes they would get in among the chickens and kill several. But nobody would say anything today, this was the owner. He could hunt where he pleased and when he pleased, it was his farm.

A Smile and a Gift

What would he be like? I was still scared of this fellow, and when he took to teasing me, I'm sure that my face turned red. When they had talked for a while, he turned to go, but before he did he turned and with a smile handed me a bright new copper penny.

I held it tightly in my hand as he and his bird dogs headed across the creek on the way to the barn and his car. A penny! A bright new copper penny! It doesn't mean anything today, but in those days it would buy two pieces of cheap bubble gum or one good stick of candy. You could even get a penny's worth of some of the mixed candy. It wasn't much candy, but it made a bulge in a little brown paper sack.

I hadn't much liked Mr. Griffith before that day, but today he seemed to be a fellow that knew about the heart of a little boy. It isn't the big things that always matter in life, it is the recognition of those things that others don't seem to notice. Things like a woman coming to a well at noon, fishermen mending nets by the seashore, a lonely tax collector sitting in a sycamore tree, or a tow-headed boy sitting on an old rail fence. Somehow he wanted to leave something with me - a smile, a gift, and a memory. These are three things that we can always leave with anyone wherever we meet them, a smile, a gift, and a memory.

A Penny to Spend

I carried the bright new copper penny safely home in my deepest pocket, along with the other things a boy might carry, marbles, a cheap knife or one that had been discarded because every blade was broken except one, and of course a few good choice stones for my sling shot. No boy should be without a few good smooth stones.

Mom would have to hear my story. It is always important to be able to tell someone about your good fortune. My penny lay on the dresser for a few days, while I was trying to decide how to spend it. I knew that I must share with my brother Jake, so I tried to think of the biggest amount of candy you could buy for a penny.

The bright new penny spent the week on the dresser. I couldn't say it was burning a hole in my pocket, but it was getting very warm on the dresser. Saturday was coming and we would soon be headed to town.

The Candy Counter

In my mind, I could already see the candy counter at Nickel's store. It was tiptoe high off the floor, and its smooth rounded glass ended in a small wooden top. It was full of the nicest, sweetest things in the world. Sometimes the store would even have open stick candy - the kind without a wrapper.

Saturday arrived, and in clean overalls and shirts, we loaded up in the pickup and headed for town. I had one bright new copper penny to spend. I opted for the two unwrapped sticks of candy, one for Jake and one for me. The bright new copper penny was in the grocer's till, but I had two candy sticks in a brown paper bag. The exchange seemed fair to me, and I was happy.

Making A Friend and A Memory

It is surprising what good thoughts about a person that the gift of a bright new copper penny could bring. I never saw the gentlemen but a few times, but I had lost my fear of him altogether. A man with a smile and the gift of a bright new copper penny had made a friend and a memory that would last for a lifetime.

Jesus said to make friends with the unrighteous mammon, to help a neighbor or someone in need. And if you are out hunting and find a little tow-headed boy wearing overalls and sitting on an old rail fence, I would suggest that you give him a smile and a bright new copper penny and make a lasting memory for both of you.

The Hay Baler

A Short Story by Dr. Harry E. Carr

Hay Baling

We always had some hay to mow ourselves. It was fun mowing the hay. We had McCormick mowers with a six-foot sickle on the right side. The mower had triangular shaped cutting blade riveted to a long sickle bar that moved back and forth between larger pointed guards with a sharp cutting edge on either side. The mechanism worked by the drive wheel of the mower. A pitman wheel and a wooden bar moved the sickle back and forth about four or five inches, cutting a six-foot swath in the standing hay.

The mower moved as fast as a good team could walk, except in very heavy hay with weeds in it. I always tried to watch for young rabbits or quail nests with those tiny speckled eggs, but most of them moved quickly out of the way. I confess that when I overtook a snake of any variety, I made no attempt to dodge it. Decapitation was more of what I had in mind.

Haying by Shares

I enjoyed mowing good clover hay or Timothy hay. In those days, we didn't have alfalfa or any other better quality of hay, unless we took on some hay to mow, rake, and bail on shares. I never quite liked the idea of the sharecropper, we did all the work but the owner received one-third of everything, including the hay. This included putting the other man's hay into the barn loft.

Preparation For Baling

Bailing hay was not the easiest of jobs. After mowing the hay, we let it cure for a day or so then it was raked with a horse drawn rake. Two horses pulled the rake. It had a special seat and a trip. The way it was suppose to work was that each time you passed over the windrow, you pushed the release with your foot and the mechanism would raise the tines and drop the hay into the row. Sometimes it didn't work and a lever about thirty inches long had to be grabbed and shoved down, this would manually dump the hay. I've dumped more hay with the lever than with the trip, which never seemed to work. Hay rakes make lots of noise, moving along the ground with each individual tine digging in. Grandpa always insisted that the hay be put into miniature stacks, which we called shocks. It seemed useless to me, but then I wasn't in charge of anything but a pitchfork. Soon, little shocks of hay each about six-foot high and about the same in diameter dotted the hay field. I always hoped for a good pair of shoes, for hay stubble can ruin your foot. Sometimes the soles were thin and I got punched anyway. We were ready for the bailer.

A Real Hay Baler

The baler wasn't all that heavy, a good team could pull it over level or slightly elevated roadways. Raines Hill (where Grandpa lived) was more than a quarter mile long and ended at Three Mile Creek, it was very steep and made a turn about two-thirds of the way down. The hill was covered with gravel with two worn and packed tracks winding down the hillside. Loose gravel would roll into the packed tracks crunching under the wheels and sometimes rolling under the firmly planted feet of the horses, serving as the brakes on the machine. It was the breeching (that is the back of the harness that goes across the rump of the horse) that was used by the horses to hold back a heavy load or to move the wagon or baler backward.

The baler was just too much for one team to hold back, a jointed tongue, which was good for pulling, wasn't worth a dime in holding back a load. Most of those temporary tongues simply hooked in the end of the stationary tongue and when backward pressure was put on it, the tongue simply jumped out of socket. There was no brake on the rig that I could see.

Iron Brake Shoes

A heavy pair of slightly curved metal weights lay on the baler, and a short chain with a hook was attached to one side of each one. They were about five or six inches wide and about fifteen or sixteen inches long. I had never seen these used until today, each was attached to the baler by the short chains just in front of the rear wheels.

Grandpa and I set and held the metal strips in front of the rear wheels. Grandpa spoke to the horses and they moved the baler forward until each rear wheel rested in the shoes.

These were iron brake shoes, the wheels were locked inside and the bottom of the brakes had a metal strip that slid along the ground. The team would be pulling slightly all the way down the hill with the wheels locked securely in the metal brakes.

I was a boy of questions, "What did you do before you had the iron shoes?" I boldly asked. "Well son, we just took a chain and tied the wheels together under the baler. It worked just as well and sometimes was less trouble." However, it was hard on the wheels to drag on the hill and there is always a risk that a wheel could be sprung, and they were expensive to buy.

Setting a Baler

The baler was usually positioned as near to the center of the field as possible; however, it did need a level place. Once in place, the teams were unhitched and moved away. We had a baler jack that was shaped like a large A, two wooden legs supported the jack and a winch with a chain came down from the top. The jack was raised and lower by a handle that was fixed on the top. It was a very tedious business, raising and lowering that baler. The slightest move could knock the jack over. It was a delicate balancing act every time you took off a wheel. All four wheels had to be removed, letting the baler rest firmly on the ground.

The baler was staked down by driving Model T axles crisscross over the baler axles. It was hard work, but necessary to keep the baler stationary during the baling operation. A short tongue was hitched to the gear mechanism on the front of the baler. A team of horses would furnish the power for the baler by walking in a circle, pulling the gears that caused two long rods to move. One raised and lowered the plunger, which was a device that drove the hay into the baler. The other operated the device that shoved the hay through the baler. The hay came through on its side, and the baler channel became smaller as it approached the end of the baler, compressing the hay tightly into bales.

Each bale was held with two wires. A loop was on one end of the wire and the other end was straight. A wooden block was placed between each bale with slots for the wires of the following bales. From the punching side of the baler, the wooden blocks were shoved out under the giant plunger and held by a single wire. The force of the plunger knocked it down into the channel upright between each bale.

On the other side, the wire tier tied the wires, leaving a little room for their expansion as they were nearing the baler's end. As each bale came out of the baler, the tier would lay it on the set of scales that had been set and balanced for the purpose. Bales were weighed two at a time and the weight was properly recorded in the record book.

Hay was bailed by the ton, whether it was for a local farmer or we were storing it in the barn. We did not divide hay by the bale but by weight. Grandpa's bales always ran heavy, not less than eighty-five and not more than one hundred pounds. That way you did not waste too much wire. Wire was expensive and Grandpa was not one to waste money.

Bring the Hay to the Baler

Grandpa, if he prepared the hay, would first rake the mowed hay into windrows and then mount it up into little stacks that we called shocks. They were about six feet high and probably the same in diameter. They would dot a field like tepees in an Indian camp.

Now they must be brought to the baler. We had two ways of bringing them in. Sometimes we used a rope that was tied in the last ring of the trace chain on the harness of the horse. We would run around the shock, kicking the rope under it with our feet, then jump on the shock and drive the horse to the baler, while scooting the shock on the ground. When the shock was at the baler, they simply pulled the quick knot, releasing the rope, and then we were on our way back to the field. However, this was difficult for me, I wasn't hardly heavy enough to hold the shock together.

I liked the sled; its wooden runners became bright and slick on the stubble of the hayfield. The sled was loaded with the shocks and driven to the baler. Two men would place a pitchfork on either side in the front of the sled, and the horses were driven forward, pulling the sled out from under the mound of hay.

Grandpa always fed the baler. He could stand all day in his long sleeve flannel shirt buttoned at the collar, wearing his old felt hat and bib overalls, and throw hay into that baler. Heat, dust, or allergies never seemed to have any effect on him. He was one of the hardest workers I knew and he demanded the same for all those who worked for him, sons and grandsons alike.

Lunch in the Hayfield

The days were hot and long. The dust kicked up from the tracks made by the horses powering the baler and the dust from the hay would nearly stifle a person. The water bucket was visited often. Usually there was no ice, just cold water drawn from the well earlier that day.

I always looked forward to the noon hour. Usually someone would bring a lunch in a cardboard box or basket to the hayfield. There was nothing fancy in that lunch, always the same thing, cornbread, fried potatoes, a pot of beans, green onions, tomatoes, and whatever else could be found in the garden. Sometimes there was even fried chicken. We always had fresh water to drink. It was a good time and everybody was hungry. But before we ate, we removed our caps or hats and Grandpa offered prayer.

Swim in the Lake

Sometimes, in the late evening when the work was done, we would have an opportunity to stop at a lake or creek for a brief swim. It was an opportunity to leave behind the dust of the day, and to relax for a few minutes. Tomorrow we would head back to the hay field, but tonight, we would spread our pallets on the great front porch and watch the stars as we dropped off into a restful sleep.

It seemed only a short time before the sun would be up over the eastern hills. It would be time, after a good breakfast, to harness the teams and head again for the hay field.

The Hoodlums of Bear Creek Baptist Church

A Short Story by Dr. Harry E. Carr

This story was either told to me by Grandpa, Dad, or one of the men in the community. I am not absolutely sure of the location of the church nor can I verify the story as being true, but it was one of the stories that I heard in my childhood. Maybe it was told to me so that I would never cause trouble at church, but if that was the reason it was totally unnecessary, for I feared the preacher with a heavenly fear and would have crawled under my seat if he had called me down. Should that have happened, only God knew what would have happened when we got home.

The Church On The County Line Road

I will tell you the story as I remember it, but please remember I heard it as a boy long ago and I may have forgotten some of the pertinent facts. I never saw the church. It was disbanded and the building gone long before I came into the community. The small spring that furnished water for the congregation was now nothing more than a trickle tracing its small branch through the meadowland to the larger creek a quarter of a mile to the south.

The Old County Line Road had long been abandoned, and existed in only a few places where it passed by a house or ran across a field or through the woods to someone's farm. It was kept open as a convenience for the farm or a family who may have lived along it and used it as an access road.

The church that I will describe was the typical country church of that day. Based on how it was described to me, I would recognize the church. It was the same as hundreds of little churches that dotted the countryside in those days of the late nineteenth and early twentieth century, where poor but devout folks gathered to worship.

Bear Creek Baptist Church set along the Pope-Hardin County Line Road about a mile from the banks of Bear Creek. It was a small wooden frame church set along the tracks in the wilderness. Churches in those days were often covered with clapboards on the outside. They were painted when new and most were never painted again. Soon the weathered wood took on a gray tint and the worn steps creaked with age and often sagged with neglect.

Church Furniture In Country Churches

In those days, the furniture of the churches was homemade. The furniture would consist of a wood stove of some sort set in the front of the church either on the left or the right side below the raised platform where the preacher preached. There would be a series of wooden benches forming two rows with an aisle in the center, a front and a back door, and some windows on either side for light and ventilation.

The benches were constructed of one by four-inch boards that were nailed to a rough frame bench end, which formed a support for the back while serving as legs on which the bench rested. A small crack was left between each board, and as a boy, I always thought they made them that way on purpose. You see, if you didn't sit just right the boards would pinch you. There was just enough give in the seat boards between the ends and the middle leg to allow them to catch your bottom in their movement and deliver a solid pinch.

The pulpit was homemade too. A finished carpenter or cabinetmaker would make the pulpit, and it would be passed down from one generation to the next, sometimes gaining a reverence, not by use, but because some long dead ancestor had hand made it. It was called the sacred desk, the preacher's stand, and of course, the pulpit. All pulpits were roughly the same. The center was about twelve to fourteen inches wide and was four or five inches higher than either side. There was always a center shelf for storing material and sometimes a glass of water for the preacher. Sermons in those days were never shorter than one hour, and some lasted for an hour and a half.

Preachers and Preaching

Most of the old country preachers did not just stand behind the pulpit and talk, they got into the message, usually with much gesticulation. Each point was made not only with words, but was duly emphasized. Preaching was from the heart and was meant to reach the heart of the listener.

Most of these churches were supported by one family, which had become several homes. Some of the churches, although they had a formal name, were known by the name of the principle family who worshipped there. Through the years they repaired, rebuilt, furnished the fuel, and paid the preacher. Outside of that there was not much expense.

Some of the larger churches sent money to their Association of Churches to sponsor missionaries and other programs. It never was a very large amount, but then nobody had money back then. The preacher was often paid with chickens, eggs, a pig, jars of canned goods, or home cured hams or bacon.

The Ruffians

According to the story told to me, there were only five or six families in the church, but there were a half a dozen of grown boys who occasionally attended. They usually attended at revivals or when there was a dinner on the grounds. These boys were a pretty tough element. It was nothing for some of the boys to arrive at church armed with pistols or knives, which were not designed for whittling. Often fights would break out in the churchyard during worship services and several men would have to go out and stop it.

Apparently, these particular boys did not fight with one another; they found another way of entertaining themselves. They took to running off the preacher. Once inside, they would jeer and mock the preacher, talk out loud, and make fun of the worshippers. The men often threatened to report them to their parents, and sometimes even to the Sheriff. However, the Sheriff had few deputies and wasn't much help. Soon the preacher would resign and leave.

Calling A New Preacher

The boys had won again. They would leave the worshippers alone, but they were again without a preacher. Soon the church was well known throughout the other country churches, for it seemed that every time a preacher came, the same old heckling would start again. The people were praying that they would get saved or just grow up and get married. Maybe that would change them. In a pack, the followers acted just like the leader and were afraid that any reaction to his actions would look like cowardice on their part. Probably only one or two of the boys had such a wicked spirit, the others merely followed.

It became impossible to get a preacher for Bear Creek Church. The actions of ruffians became well known in the other churches and the preachers just never *"felt a call to accept the pulpit at Bear Creek Baptist Church."* The families kept the doors open but that was about all. They were afraid to have a revival. Who would come?

A Preacher From The Backwoods

This man came out of the backwoods of Kentucky. He was a Baptist and he certainly could preach. Some had heard him in a revival, and the pulpit committee invited him to Bear Creek Church to candidate. Of course, they forgot to mention the ruffians, besides they might be different because they hadn't been around for sometime now. The preacher liked the church and since he had moved into the area, he accepted the call at once. Bear Creek Church once again had a new pastor.

The Harassment Renewed

It wasn't long until the same harassment began - loud jeering, talking during the sermon, and threatening the preacher. The small congregation expected him resign, but he called the boys down and explained to them the fine points of attending church and worship. He had a kind manner about him, and it was hoped that it might just win them over. However, the next week it was just the same only it turned to violence. Some of the men who tried to control them were beaten up and they even threaten to beat up the preacher if he returned.

A Bible and Two Pistols

The next Sunday the congregation gathered, sure that they would have no preacher. The ruffians were there too, making their boast and applauding their defeat of yet another preacher. Suddenly, the preacher walked in wearing a long coat. He passed through the crowd with scarcely a word to anyone. Everyone was prepared for a resignation speech and none more prepared then the ruffians. The preacher made his way to the pulpit and laid his Bible on the stand. Then reaching into his great coat pocket, he pulled out two very large pistols laying one on either side of the pulpit. "Boys," he said, "I have come here today to preach, and these two pistols came to assure me that I would be heard. If you have any objection, speak up now or sit down and be quiet." You could hear a pin drop, or so I am told.

The End of the Reign of the Ruffians

The preacher never used the pistols. I seriously doubt if he ever intended to, but those ruffians were certainly convinced that he might and not one of them wanted to chance it. The presence of those formable weapons sure made believers out of those boys. The boys kept attending the church, mostly out of respect for a preacher, whom they could not scare with their threats nor harass into resigning. There was no more trouble out of them. There was singing, preaching, praying, and even shouting, but it was of the religious variety.

A New Day at Bear Creek Church

In time, most of the boys, now young men, were saved and became respected members of Bear Creek Baptist Church. They would laugh about that Sunday long ago, when the preacher delivered the ultimate challenge to a bunch of ruffians of whom they were a part. The preacher stayed a few years and then went on to pastor other churches, but they never forgot the preacher who tamed Bear Creek Baptist Church.

THE HOODLUMS OF BEAR CREEK BAPTIST CHURCH

The story of the preacher and his guns passed among the churches. It was told and retold and I am sure that each time it was told the ruffians got worse and the guns got bigger. But as long as Bear Creek was a church, they had no problem in finding a man, who could, *"feel the call to be their pastor."*

My First Bible

A Short Story by Dr. Harry E. Carr

Family Heritage

My Grandfather was a deacon at Bethany Church, which was located near Hicks Branch. The church was actually eight to ten miles from where we lived. Grandpa belonging there was probably more sentiment than practical in the latter years. It may have had something to do with Grandma's Dad, who had also been a deacon at this church in years gone by.

A Local Church

When we attended church, it was a church much closer to home and it was of the same denomination. It was known as Keeling Hill General Baptist. Grandpa did not own or drive a car, and distance was of great consideration. Unless Daddy went, Grandpa had to drive a team of horses and usually attended day services.

Although we did not attend church regularly, we usually attended revivals, special meetings, and of course, the Association. The Association was the annual meeting of the organization of several churches of the same denomination in a locale. The church was banded together for mutual support and to pool their resources to promote the Gospel and their own denomination. The annual Association began on Thursday afternoon and ended on Saturday at noon. Religious services with singing and preaching were held both at the daily eleven o'clock hour and every night.

There was no doubt that the family was committed to certain religious principles. Three times each day a blessing was given at each meal, no exceptions were made or accepted. There was neither swearing nor bad language permitted. You did not bet on anything at anytime regardless of the circumstances, nor were dice or cards allowed in the house.

In Defense of the Bible

My first theological argument was with the kid that lived on the next farm. The intelligence of that argument would undoubtedly have impressed people for years, had they only heard it. The fellow argued that the Bible was not the Word of God, but rather that it was just a book some men had written. In his opinion, the book was silly and worthless. His atheistic statements both frightened and then angered me. Surely if God heard him, he was in deep trouble.

I did not know why I believed the Bible to be a true religious book, maybe it was Grandma or Mother's faith or perhaps it was Grandpa's prayers and strict code of ethics. I don't know why but I just believed that the Bible was true, and I would not allow such challenges to go unchallenged. I had the "faith" of my grandparents and parents and although I could not explain it well enough to defend the position, I knew that they were right. The Bible was God's Book and that was that.

The Family Bible

Grandpa had a Bible that he often carried to church. It was a zipper Bible of which he was very proud. Although he did not read it often, it came out to go to church or to consider a passage of Scripture. Grandma did not have a Bible, because she could not read. Mother had an inexpensive Bible and there was one other Bible in the house. It was a large family Bible with family records, births, deaths, and weddings. It was kept in an old trunk in Grandpa and Grandma's bedroom. The Bible came out only to make a new entry or to check one previously made. It was very old and very delicate.

A School Program

A salesman had come to our school today, and he was offering Bible mottoes for us to sell. The mottoes were black metallic with silver lettering on them. The lettering was made by a machine imprinting them from the backside making raised lettering. Each motto was about five or six inches high by about twelve inches long. Each contained a Bible verse or a portion of a verse. They were quite attractive to hang on the wall and I found out that they were easy to sell. We had only one week to make the sales.

Amazing Things

Two things amaze me as I look back from the perspective of today. First, that you could have a Bible program in the public school. The Bible was on prominent display in the classroom and sometimes a Bible verse and prayer opened school in the morning. It all depended upon the teacher's religious convictions.

Secondly, I was completely amazed that they would allow me to participate in the program. After all, I was a little seven-year-old country boy with no experience in selling, but every child has parents and grandparents which usually are easy and ready customers.

The school must have received some form of dividend from the sale of the mottoes. I am sure it was not in monetary form, perhaps it was a piece of school equipment or some books. I really wasn't interested in that, all I could see was that nice new Bible lying on the table by the teacher's desk.

The Prize

The new Bible had caught my eye from the first. It wasn't large, probably four by six inches, but it was a full inch and a half or two inches thick. Its black covers glittered in the schoolroom light, and upon inspection it seemed to have all the important stuff, a name page, several pictures, and all the books of the Bible. It was a virtual treasure for anyone to own.

The Book of All Books

Little did I realize how important the Bible would become to me across the years, but I knew this was a book worthy of winning. There was a smaller Bible going to the second place winner. Later I learned that it was only a New Testament and this, well this one was the whole Bible.

The Creed of Caleb

I was kind of like Caleb of old, who, although he was eighty-five, wanted the mountains of Israel for his home. "I want that mountain," he would say, and I wanted that Bible more I think than anything else I ever wanted. I was determined whatever the cost and whatever the time, that it would be mine tomorrow.

School was out. Loaded with my books and as many of those mottoes as I could get, I started my sales pitch with Uncle Sam Hosick, who lived just across the road and upon the hill. They bought two, and I was on my way, or at least I thought, to success. I sold one to everybody I could; of course, Mom and Grandma each bought a motto. They chose carefully and well. I asked everyone I knew, family or otherwise, to buy one.

A Boy Salesperson

I never considered myself a good salesman, but I wanted that Bible desperately and I couldn't be bashful and win. When there was only one or two left and the choice of Bible verses was down to one or two, the sales were getting a little tougher but I was persistent. Before the evening was over, I had sold every motto in my possession, and to the best of my memory, I had taken an order for one or two extra mottoes.

The Day of Reward

I could hardly wait for the week to pass; I had sold mine to relatives and anyone else who stood still long enough. I had requested extra mottoes and sold them. I thought I was doing pretty well, but I didn't know for sure so I worried a lot. Had someone sold more than I? Would I be in second place and win the smaller award or maybe I would win nothing. The teacher never told us who was ahead, but he always smiled when I asked for more mottoes.

The week dragged slowly by or so it seemed. The school was out of mottoes; there were no more to sell. It was Friday, the day of reckoning. The motto man had returned to collect the money and pick up the unsold mottoes and present the awards. I was surprised to see several mottoes returned, some kids hadn't sold more than one or two. I confess, I was a little relieved when I saw some returning the mottoes.

The sales were complete, the count was made, and I had won. The Bible was mine! I was the proudest and happiest kid in school. It really was, in my estimation, the finest of Bibles. I realize that it was a rather inexpensive Bible by today's standards, but Bibles were not readily available and they cost far more money than we had to spare.

Telling Others About Your Win

I carried my cherished gift home like it was a diamond. It was a wonderful reward. I wanted the whole family to see what I had won. Daddy wrote my name in the front, it was my own Bible. I still have that Bible in my possession to this very day. The backs are gone and the pages show wear, but each time I hold it memories flood back. I can recall the joy

I had in winning a very special book and the pride of owning my very own Bible.

A Lasting Impression

Now if I stopped here, I would be leaving out one of the best parts of the story. Mom hung her motto on the wall over the bed in the room which Jake and I slept. It was the first verse of Psalm 23, *"The Lord is my shepherd."* Each morning I read the verse and each night I read it again by a fading lamplight before I fell asleep.

Grandma hung her motto on the living room wall just to the right of the heating stove. Each morning as we came into the living room, I read Grandma's motto, *"The Lord is my light and salvation"* a quote from the first verse of Psalm 27. These were the first two verses of the Scriptures that I memorized. They sealed themselves in my memory and found the way into my heart. I wonder how many boys or girls have learned the beginning of the Scriptures as I did, from a simple little black motto with bright silver colored letters.

In memory, I can locate the mottoes, position them on the wall, and read them again. The plaques are long gone, but *"the word of God lives and abideth forever."* I Peter 1:23b

Gathering Wild Nuts For Winter

A Short Story by Dr. Harry E. Carr

For The Love Of Nuts

As a family, we loved all kinds of nuts; however, we never bought them at the store except at Christmas time. Although I can say, we did on occasion buy peanuts in the shell from the grocery story. They were quite reasonably priced just after harvest.

At Christmas every grocery store in town or in the countryside had Christmas nuts displayed in open burlap bags, no nuts were prepackaged in those days. The tops of each burlap bag were carefully rolled down to better display the nuts. The usual nuts were English walnuts, pecans, Brazil nuts, and hazelnuts. I can never remember any other kind, maybe because these were the only ones we ever bought.

The nuts, along with some candy and citrus fruit, made up the children's Christmas menu. And it was, in my opinion, a very good menu. Who could ask for more?

Nuts Growing in the Wild

We lived in the Shawnee National Forest area of Southern Illinois. Every farm had its own woodland, and in any direction you looked there were trees and more trees. Several of the older farms had been purchased by the Forest Service of the Federal Government and reverted back to woodlands. Some of the fields had been planted with pines; however, most were still hardwoods. Even when forests were cut for timber, it was never a "clear cut" and within a few years the trees had taken over again.

In the multiplied woodlands there were a lot of nut bearing trees. The problem was finding them and sometimes remembering where they were. You could always pick up nuts on the state or government owned lands, and many of the other landowners did not care if you picked up nuts from their woods. The "No Trespassing" signs so common today were uncommon in those times. Most farmers could care less about two boys wandering around in the woods. But we pretty much stayed at home; there were usually plenty of nuts to find on our own property.

The only wild nuts with which we were familiar were the black walnuts, hickory nuts, hazelnuts, and pecans. While they were quite common, not all the trees produced enough nuts to fool with gathering them. Most people picked up a few nuts from trees that were convenient and where nuts were easy to gather.

Pecans, at least where they grew in abundance, seemed to be the exception. Property owners gathered them more seriously. Pecan trees were more abundant along creek and riverbanks; however, they might be found anywhere in an open field. Daddy said that the trees that produced the largest pecan harvest in our area grew in the Shawnee bottoms, near the little Ohio River city of Shawneetown. However, the trees were on privately owned land and few people, to my knowledge, had the opportunity of gathering them. One of the dreams of my childhood was to gather nuts from these trees, probably because of what Dad had said about them.

Hunting For Pecan Trees

Usually pecan trees grew in the meadows near a creek or spring branch. Frequently they grew near the edge of the woods, but I have never seen a pecan tree growing deep within the woodlands. The nuts from these pecan trees were smaller and so was the harvest. Jake and I hunted for any nut tree, but a pecan tree was a great find. Nuts depended on the weather, soil, and environment; therefore, in some years nuts were plentiful and in others there were hardly any nuts at all.

One good pecan tree could make for several pleasant winter evenings around the heating stove cracking nuts. Sometimes the kernels would be picked out and put in cakes or the icing on the cake, and sometimes they were baked into cookies or into candy. Candy was usually made with cocoa, milk, sugar, and flavoring. Nuts of any variety were a great addition to both the candy and cookies.

Black Walnuts

Black walnut trees were everywhere, but they too had good and bad seasons. Removing the outer shell from the walnut was a difficult task. If they were too green, the juice stained both hands and clothing alike. Once out of the shell, the black walnut would need to dry a few days before eating. They too were not only a part of a good family evening, but also a great ingredient for cakes, cookies, and candy.

You might find walnut trees almost anywhere, but the best was always at the edge of the woods. However, the squirrels also found them very attractive. I have killed several squirrels, especially the red fox squirrels, feeding in walnut trees. However, in my honest opinion, squirrels prefer hickory nuts and acorns.

Hazelnuts

Hazelnuts were of the smaller variety. They were easy to crack, but they contained only one round kernel. These nuts were nothing like the big cultured filbert nuts of today, but in my opinion, they were far more tasty and of a better quality. Uncle Sam, mother's uncle from Shawnee Hollar, gave Jake and I a bag of hazelnuts every fall. He had laboriously harvested them, for he had a crippled leg and any walking was a real chore for him. He must have covered several acres to gather that many nuts. So I considered the five-pound bag of hazelnuts a generous gift of love. He had little else that he could give. Somehow I wish he knew how much that little bag of nuts meant to me.

He and his wife had no children; they lived in a little two-room shack deep within the hollar. They carried water from a spring down the hill and across the road from their house. They walked to the store or caught a ride into the little town to shop.

Wild hazelnuts grew on a cluster of bushes four to six feet high, usually at the edge of the field or in a fencerow. The squirrels would help harvest these as well; however, their balance on the small bushes was always precarious. Hunting squirrels on the bushes took a good shot and lots of patience.

Again, knowing where hazelnut bushes were was imperative to harvesting the nuts. It was also helpful to keep an eye on the coming harvest, lest you lose them all to the varmints. Any addition we could add to the few pounds given to us by Uncle Sam was welcomed and enjoyed.

Preparation For The Cold Winter

I know today we don't have to be concerned about a food supply for the winter, but it was vastly different in those days. We had to lay up as many things as possible during the summer and fall months for the winter that was soon to come. Of course, some of the things we prepared may have been available in the better grocery stores, but it was not convenient to us nor did we have the money to buy them even if they were.

Unnecessary food or luxury foods were only seasonal; we made do with what we had. So in the summer we picked and canned blackberries, a hundred and fifty or more quarts were considered just barely enough. Peaches from the orchards in the southern part of the state were gathered and canned. We bought only the overripe peaches that had fallen off the trees and were lying on the ground. They were cold packed. To cold pack the peaches, the peeled peaches were placed in a jar with syrup made of sugar and water and were then sealed. The filled jars were set in a number two washtub, which was placed on stones and then fired until the peaches were properly "cold-packed".

GATHERING WILD NUTS FOR WINTER

Potatoes were hilled up. A hole was first dug, filled with straw or hay, the potatoes were placed in it, and then they were covered with more straw, and then finally covered with a mound of dirt. These would be dug into during the winter. Cabbage was made into kraut. Granny always peeled the cabbage cores and placed those in the kraut jar, a huge store or earthware container that would hold five or six gallons. I liked the kraut, but the cabbage cores were a treat that I enjoyed very much.

Several hogs were killed and the meat was cured with white salt and stored in the smokehouse. Sausage was made by grinding the pork mixed with fat and adding pepper, sage, salt, and other spices. Since we had no other way to keep the sausage, it was fried and placed in fruit jars covered with hot grease and sealed to be opened later.

Some of the pork loin was also sliced and fried and sealed the same way. What a treat when Grandma or Mom opened a quart jar of the pork loin, placed them in homemade dressing, and baked them in the oven!

If gathering nuts was to be done, then it depended on Jake and I. Of course, others gave encouragement and told of the location of the trees that they knew about. The whole family enjoyed the nuts as much as we did.

Hickory Nuts

The most abundant of all nuts for us were the hickory nuts. They came in a variety of sizes, shapes, and shells. The shells all looked similar; however, some were very hard and very thick and the kernels were small. Now it seemed that the squirrels liked these best of all. One old and very tall hickory tree grew in our back woods, from which I have killed my limit of squirrels on many a Saturday morning during hunting season. The tree had very small and very hard hickory nuts and always had plenty of them.

However, the squirrels seemed to like them best of all. During squirrel hunting season, I would slip into the woods before daylight, sit quietly near the old hickory, and listen as the squirrels gathered into the tree to feed in the dark of the early morning. When the first rays of daylight came, I would usually stand in one place, kill my limit of five squirrels, and be back home, three quarters of a mile away, for breakfast before nine o'clock.

The best hickory nuts were found on the "scaly bark" hickory trees. The nuts varied in size but almost all had a thin shell and large kernels. There were much larger hickory nuts, but they had a very thick shell and a very small kernel.

The "scaly bark" nuts were the very best. To know where there was a tree or two was usually enough for the winter. In the late fall, the ripe nuts fell to the ground and were free of their outer fiber shell. Most of the fiber shells were broken in the fall. The bare hickory nuts lay on the ground scattered among the fallen leaves of autumn.

Finding The Large Scaly Bark Trees

The new farm to which we had just moved was just waiting to be explored. Mom did not worry about us when we were out in the field or the woods. She did not even worry about us when we took our cane fishing poles and a can of worms and headed for the creek or pond. She only worried when we went swimming. Her old adage was, "Don't go in the water until you learn how to swim." No amount of persuasive argument could show her how illogical her reasoning was. On this one, she was planted like a tree by the water and would not be moved.

We did swim of course, but we waited until our hair dried before we came home. We dared not lie about it, we just didn't mention that we had taken a dip in the creek. I think she knew, but just ignored it. We were back safe, and for the moment, that was all that really mattered to her.

Two Dirt Roads

Behind the barn on the new farm was a large pasture field composed of about twenty or more acres. A quarter mile away the pastureland merged into the woods. It had two roads that wound through it, one of the roads ran along the hill top and led to uncle Joe Kitter's homestead and then beyond to a much larger farm. I believe that at one time that section may have been one of the main roads of the area; however, now it was nothing more than a convenience road that had been long forgotten by most people. The lower road ran through the hollow between the two small hills and through the very heart of the woods. Tall trees lined each side of the road as it wound among them on the way to the field that lay beyond.

The Back Field

The field was probably sixty or more acres with the eastern hillside still new ground. Most of it was still covered with brush and fallen trees. We opened up a little more each time we plowed the field. The new ground slopped away into the more fertile bottomland, which had a small spring branch that came from the east, made a right turn, and separated the field into three sections. The small branch was the dividing line for plowing. If the entire field was plowed, it was plowed on three sides of that branch. One of the lines was only imaginary, but it ran from the property line and joined that branch where it then made a right curve and headed south to the woods lot.

Things To Do and Places To Be

We were never bored as kids, there was too much to see and do in our spare time, and there were always chores in the morning and evening. In planting and harvest season we were kept busy, but beyond that we were pretty much on our own. We played and searched the woods for all the edible things. Even persimmon trees were located there. They were pretty good eating, and even some animals liked them very much. You did not eat a persimmon until after the first heavy frost. If you tried to eat them green, your mouth would feel puckered for a week.

Paw-Paw Trees

Down in the swamp area, there were a few paw-paw bushes but I never developed any taste for them. Mayflowers also grew over the woods and produced a yellow small lemon size fruit. I never cared for them either; however, they were edible.

The East Wood Lot

Black walnut trees grew by the road leading from the main road into the barn lot, and it seems that I can remember two others on the hillside near the east wood lot. It was in this wood lot that I found the big black oak bee tree, which Dad and I cut down with the help of my uncles. Uncle Bill was in the army somewhere in the South Pacific; these were the days of World War II. At every Sunday's family gathering, his name was always mentioned and news about him was eagerly shared. He was the youngest of Dad's brothers and sisters and was the favorite of the family. Not only because he was away, but because of his personality.

Five Scaly Barks in a Row

It is easy to spot a scaly bark hickory nut tree. Their loose slabs of bark stands out in contrast with the tight fitting bark of the harder hickory nut trees. However, every scaly bark hickory nut tree was not a productive one. There were two ways you could tell about the productivity of a tree. One was to check the ground litter under the tree, there should be hulls and probably some nuts left over from last year. The other way was to check the trees in late summer and early fall for their present crop. At that time there should be a good harvest on the trees.

There they were at the edge of the woods, five scaly bark hickory nut trees stood in a row. No one could have planted them any straighter than they were. They were just far enough away from the main woods to make them a little inconvenient for the squirrels and they preferred the harder nuts anyway.

The nuts even on these scaly barks differed greatly. Some were larger, some were almost square with rounded corners, while others were longer. Even the thickness of the nut varied, but they were all good with thin shells and large kernels. Not all of these trees were productive, but there were three trees you could count on every year. The nuts from these trees would be enough to nearly fill a burlap bag.

We always watched for those nuts that had a tiny hole in the bottom. You see, that is where a worm had entered or exited, and so you just threw those away. Occasionally you might find a bad nut when you cracked them, but they were very few indeed.

Clothes Irons and Horse Shoe Nails

These were not nuts you could crack with nut crackers, besides that, we did not own any such instruments. We gathered around the heating stove in the winter, put a clothes iron upside down on our lap, and cracked the nuts with a small hammer. Clothes irons were flat heavy metal perhaps five to eight ounces in weight with a metal handle extending above it. The iron was heated on the stove until very hot, then using a potholder, the iron was carried to the ironing board to iron or press clothes.

But that flat bottom iron sure made a nice anvil to crack nuts on. However, it was not wise to hit the iron with the hammer as it might leave an imprint and you could get into serious trouble for that.

Retrieving the "Goodies"

Once the nut was cracked, we needed a pick and again we improvised. We would use a horseshoe nail; the nail was used to nail horseshoes on the horses. Each nail was about two and a half inches long; however, they did come in different sizes and lengths. Grandpa usually had two or three different sizes of horseshoe nails in his horse shoeing toolbox. The nails were sized according to the shoe and the size of the horse's foot. The nails had a large strange shaped head that fit into the grove of the horseshoe so they would not wear off. The nail was flat and very sharp; excellent for digging out those stubborn and reluctant goodies.

In fact, I often carried a horseshoe nail in my pocket and if available, a few nuts in the other pocket. At the shop or barn you could always find a hammer and have a snack anytime. There was just one danger in this, if you have never seen or held a horse shoe nail you would know that the point is very sharp, much sharper than a common nail and it would pick your leg if you were not careful. The solution, brad the nail just a little on the blacksmiths shop anvil, but not too much or it would not dig out the best parts of the kernel.

Two Boys and Memories

Those days are nothing more than memories of a boyhood long gone and never to return. But those were good days, happy days when just a couple of boys found things to do, nuts to eat, and places to play. There were woods and fields and barns and creeks to explore, and on any given day a hundred things to do. My brother and I spoke recently of special memories of those days and evenings around the old stove glowing red with heat, cracking nuts, and listening to Grandpa's stories.

GATHERING WILD NUTS
FOR WINTER

Gone are the days and the faces of childhood but richly live the memories in my heart, and occasionally I relive them again.

A Country Boy Meets Jesus

A Short Story by Dr. Harry E. Carr

A New Farm

We had moved for the first time in my life. Gone were the familiar things of the early years, a new home, a new school, and new places to explore. We soon made friends with some of the boys down the road, and within a year or so we were comfortable with our new home. These stories will be written from events of both homesteads. Again the farm was that of a sharecropper. It had a bigger house than the other, but the barn was much smaller.

In A Little Country Church

It was just a little church set by the side of where the main road used to run. When the paved highway came through, it was a half of a mile west of the church. The old roadway was abandoned beyond the church, it was only a gravel road that ran through the backwoods and joined with Illinois route 146, the link between Elizabethtown and Golconda. To my knowledge, the church was the last building before the link was made with the route.

Services were held on the first and third weekends, and the services were all weekend long. Saturday night we met at seven and Sunday morning at eleven and again Sunday night at seven. On the other weekends there were no regular services, with the exception of a small Sunday school class usually conducted by a neighboring girl just a year older than I was. She later became my Aunt Ellen. Sometimes she stopped by and took us with her to Sunday school.

Sunday school literature was extremely limited but there was always a supply for the "card" class. Material for the "card" class consisted of a three by five card with a picture on the front and the Bible story written on the back. The teacher simply held the card up and then read the story on the back. I am afraid that on any given Sunday we did not get much more training than the information on this simple little card.

Seating Arrangements in the Church

The church had a wooden floor that sloped all the way to the front. The pulpit and choir area were raised about eight inches above the floor level. Anything that would roll, a marble or coin, if dropped in the back would roll all the way to the front, unless it hit someone's foot.

The men usually sat on the left side of the church and the women on the right; however, this was not a solid rule and some set as families. Teens usually set with the "sinners" towards the back unless the parents made them set nearer to the front. There was an Amen corner for both the men and the women. There were three benches on either side of the front. The older men sat on the left facing the women who sat on the right. The same number of seats were upon the platform, and again, the same protocol was observed in the choir.

I thought these were the hardest people in the world. Besides being somewhat afraid of them, I was sure that they did not like me at all. I can still remember Uncle Will seated on the front seat leaning forward and resting both his hands and often his head on his cane. Uncle Andrew set alone in the middle seat and Uncle Ben in the back. The pastor's wife usually sat in the front row on the women's side joined by one or more of the ladies. I thought that they were very very old. They probably were no more than fifty or in their early sixties, but then that seemed very old to me.

The Church and Revival

The church had called an evangelist from a nearby city and although I had not seen him before, I was really impressed. I am afraid that I wasn't impressed with the preaching, but with his life before he was saved. However, the message was getting through I am sure. I think I was far more impressed with our pastor, whose hair was white as snow and who spoke with a lisp, but his voice was firm, confident, and sure. He was deeply committed to his faith in Christ and his ministry to the local church.

Revivals in those days were a minimum of two weeks and sometimes even longer. We went every night. For some reason, the teens were sitting about four rows from the front on the left side of the church. The church was small and you could not talk or cut up very much. Everyone could see and hear you, so you were "sorta" forced into listening.

I confess that I knew very little about the Bible and even less on how to become a Christian. Like so many others, I just assumed that if you were in a Christian family you were a Christian.

As the revival progressed I was exposed to more and more solid preaching and great songs of faith. Then one night, in the midst of the invitation, the pastor walked back to the bench where the teens were sitting. He spoke quietly to some of the teens and although he wasn't talking to me, I heard every word he said. I never felt so bad in all my life. For the first time, I realized that I was a sinner, lost without any hope of heaven, and doomed for hell. I didn't know much, but there was one thing that I was sure of, I did not want to go to hell.

The Mourner's Bench

The pastor stopped in front of me and quietly said, "Come and go with me." I didn't know for sure where we were going but I sure wasn't going to miss it. In our church, we turned a seat around facing the congregation, which was often called the "mourners" bench. This phrase comes from an old Methodist practice. When in a meeting, a person who wanted to be saved came and sat on the bench and mourned for his sins for one or more days or nights. The mourner stayed as many times as he or the preacher thought necessary to properly mourn for his sins, and afterwards he received Christ.

This process was totally theologically unsound and was not practiced in the church I was attending. The seat served only as a place to kneel and pray. I did not get to the front bench since the whole front was filled with people praying. Instead, I knelt by the front bench in the old men's section.

Receiving Christ

I did not know what to do. Then from somewhere Grandma found me. Kneeling beside me, she told me all she knew, and to the very best of knowledge, I believed and trusted Jesus to be my Saviour. I was just a little boy, so I did not make a very big stir to many, but do you know who were the first to welcome me into the family of God. You're right. It was the old men and women who hugged me and bid me welcome. If I had known my conversion would have made such a change in their life, I would have been saved much earlier. They became my dearest friends and I cherish their memories to this very day.

Learning The Do's and Don'ts

The very first things I heard were the things that I as a Christian should not do. Well meaning but frightening advice, for I felt very weak as a new believer. I was looking for encouragement and it came on the very next Sunday.

Sunday the evangelist was gone and the pastor was back in the pulpit. His dear wife was seated in her regular place, but today she held on her lap, along with her Bible, a new Bible. Although others were saved in that revival, I knew that Bible was for me. I didn't know how I knew, I just knew. After church that day, our pastor and his wife presented that Bible to me. There was no explanation given for the presentation, it was just made and that was all. Although I was grateful, I had great wonder about it.

The next February, the church held a baptizing in Three Mile Creek and I was among those being baptized. The Sunday began as a beautiful day but by noon it was cold and sleeting; however, the scheduled baptizing went on. I was shivering when I came out of the cold water; Grandma gave me her coat to wear the mile or so to the house and a warm change of clothing.

About the Bible

After I had announced my call into the ministry, I had an opportunity to visit that former pastor and his wife in their home. There I learned about that strange Sunday morning so long ago. You see, Uncle Joe had told his good wife, "that boy will be called to preach and you and I are going to buy him his first Bible." Now the Bible wasn't expensive by today's standard, but it became and is still today, very valuable to me. It is always good to have someone believe in you and to challenge you to be your very best.

Treasure Books of Memory

The Bible rests today beside the first Bible I ever had, which I had earned, and by the Bible given to me when I was ordained into the ministry. There is another book that rests with these three books, and you should know that it too came in an unusual way.

As a young preacher without formal training, I was studying but I did not know how to outline a message. I had never seen a book on sermon outlines or how to study. One night as my wife, daughter, and I returned home from a small church where I had preached, I saw a book lying in the middle of the road. I always had an interest in books. Although the denomination which I was in at the time did not believe in formal training nor in outlining sermons, I knew that if I was to ever preach, I must first learn.

The book had captured my attention. There was no traffic on the road, so I turned around and went back to retrieve the book. It was a new hardbound copy of Charles H. Spurgeon's Sermon Notes. Unmarked and unsigned, the book was brand new. What a treasure God had sent me! Where did the book come from? I do not know. It was lying just over the hill on a state route late at night, how unlikely that was. Did God just feel sorry for a young preacher who was desperate to learn? It was more precious than gold to me and I believe to the people that I would pastor.

Books to Remember

Each Bible was a treasure. Each with its own message, and each with a memory to be remembered. And so it was that the wonderful book of Sturgeon's Outlines became a book with worn pages, added notes, and learned sermons. It, along with the Bible, shaped those early days of my ministry and taught a boy how to be a preacher.

The Best Fly Trap in Town

A Short Story by Dr. Harry E. Carr

He was a very large man. As a boy, I often saw him passing by Dad's gristmill, visiting with someone in the alley or doing something on the back porch of his house. Although there seemed to be ample ground available for a vegetable garden, I never knew him to plant or work a garden. Maybe there were a few loose plants around the house, but nothing more.

The Relief Truck

Once every two weeks, or was it weekly or monthly, I don't really remember how often it was that the big Government Relief truck came to town. People would be on the square waiting for it long before it arrived and opened for business. It wasn't just the people of the town who came to meet the truck, a few came but not many, most of those who came were from the surrounding countryside, where poverty had crushed the hopes of the people.

In the early morning, they arrived in town. They came with their long white meal sacks. A meal sack was a heavy tightly woven cotton bag. It was probably eighteen to twenty inches in diameter and a full five feet long. It was made to put flour or meal in both sides and had a place in the middle where it could lay over the withers of the horse or mule or across or behind the saddle and would not slide off on the way home.

Parked On Main Street

The big truck had a very large box covered bed. It seemed to be always painted white. The entire back of the huge enclosure would open for the distribution of the goods it contained. The truck would park just off the main street in town, which was in reality a state route located just above Hosick's hardware store. On the high bank just beside the truck, perched upon a small partial of land that had been salvaged by building a high stone retainer wall, sat the dentist office.

The Stores On Courthouse Hill

The sidewalk on the east side of the street passed the truck on the right and continued on up Courthouse Hill ending at

Winter's store at the top of the hill. Just across the street from Winter's store was Jackson's General Store. Jackson's store was one of the popular shopping places for the family. Sometimes one of my twin uncles, who were just small boys, would be sent by horseback to the store to buy something. Usually it was a quarters worth of Great Northern beans, a pound or two of sugar (sugar came in fifty or hundred pound bags and was weighed out by the pound), a pound of coffee, or a twenty-five pound bag of flour.

Curb Side Service

They would wait patiently on the horse or mule until they were notice by Mr. Jackson or his wife, who would then come out of the store, take the order and their money, fill the order and bring it and the change back to the boys. They didn't dismount. Why? If the boys got off the horse, it was very difficult to remount. So they just sat and waited. This curbside service was new for the day and endeared the store and its owners to Uncle Bill and Uncle Abe. This is a part of the story shared with me by Uncle Bill in a recent conversation.

The Mounting Stone at Henry's Store

There was a mounting block consisting of a very large stone located at the street corner by the east side of Henry's store. I was told it was for ladies who used to ride to the store sidesaddle; however, it was just as handy for a short boy riding a tall horse without a saddle. Saddles cost money and we seldom owned one. Later we came into possession of two saddles, a McClellan and a small Texas saddle with fenders and a horn.

Relief Came in Many Packages

What wonderful things came in the back of the Relief Truck! Rice, oats, cheese, prunes, raisins, peanut butter, oranges, or grapefruit in season, crackers, flour, meal, and an assortment of things that never graced our table. I admit that I was often envious of those who came with their bags ready to receive whatever was available, and as a boy I had some difficulty with the staunch resolve of the family to make their own way.

Refusing Government Help

I do not believe for a moment that Grandpa or Daddy thought it wrong for those people who were desperate in their poverty to receive aid; however, we were not desperate. Well, they weren't but sometimes I thought I was. It was years before I realized the fierce pride and loyalty they had to self-reliance and hard work.

As with every program designed to help people, there were those who took advantage of this new "help" program. Some because they were too lazy to work, others for convenience sake, but most because they really needed help. It would be unfair of me to judge those who came; however, as a boy I am sure that I did.

The Scarcity of Work

I am sure that in those days some might have been unable to work, obviously most did not have a job because none were available. A farm hand would be hired during planting or harvest season and then only by a family who did not have enough children to get the job done. The work was seasonal and the pay extremely poor, only seventy-five cents to a dollar a day with one or two meals pitched in. You did not turn anyone away from your table whether a visitor or an employee.

The Mines

There was no major industry in the county except the fluorspar mines in the south or the coal mines in the counties just north and east of us. The pay was very low and the jobs for the most part were very hazardous. However, it was the only decent paying job around anywhere

Working at the Sawmill

There were also a few sawmills around the countryside and periodically a job would open up and you could get a few days work. Ward's sawmill, the closest one to where we lived, was on the other side of Hosick Creek, just a little north but mostly east of Basset school. The logs, eight to ten feet long, had been brought from the woods and corded so they could be easily rolled into the mill.

The logs were loaded one at a time on the saw carriage, which was pulled past the saw and returned by a series of cables. The man on the carriage could determine the speed of the saw pass, the thickness of the next board, or reverse the carriage should the log get pinched in the saw. The log was fastened to the carriage by two heavy sharp "dogs" located at either end of the carriage. As soon as the log passed back behind the saw, he was busy ratcheting the log over to expose the depth of the new board.

Once the board was cut off, it dropped onto a short conveyor made of steel rollers which usually ran only a few feet beyond the saw, from then on the work was done by hand. Each board had to be hand carried and stacked on the lumber pile according to it size and shape. A smaller saw, driven by a separate belt, was used to cut wood from the slab and scrap pile for firewood for the boiler.

The Steam Engine

At Ward's Mill, power for the entire sawmill was supplied by one old steam engine. The engine could be mobile, for it was on wheels. The rear wheels were about five-foot high and the front wheels were smaller with a steel bead running down the middle of the iron wheel. If the occasion demanded a move, the same engine used to furnish power for machinery could be transferred to power the wheels. Under its own power the machine could be driven down the road to another place. It probably had the maddening speed of five to ten miles an hour depending upon the head of steam.

Guiding it was almost an impossible task, no one had ever heard of rack and pinion steering. A man of strength and determination must wrestle the iron steering wheel. So once the steam engine was set, it usually stayed unless it was one used to operate a wheat or oat thresher. If it was, then frequent moving was made from farm to farm.

As long as I could remember, this same steam engine had set at Wards and was never moved. Sales from a sawmill depended on farms and buildings. Most of the rough lumber was not used for housing, except among the very poor. It also depended upon the mining industry, which needed lumber for both the underground as well as surface construction.

How The Steam Engine Worked

Water was stored in the great reservoir and heated by the crackling of the wood in the boiler. The steam raised by using firewood cut from the slab pile (a slab is the bark side of the log and the first board cut from the log on all four sides).

The old steam engine leaked steam from almost every fitting as well as the exhaust of the engine. It was a one-man job to keep a head of steam on the old boiler. A steady stream of cut slabs had to be fed into the firebox to keep the water hot and the steam flowing to the steam motor.

The pay at the sawmill was lower than that of the mine, probably something like ten to fifteen dollars a week depending upon the position you held. Usually in the small sawmills, the whole crew went to the woods, cut the trees, cut off the logs, hauled them to the mill, and then processed them into boards or into other types of lumber. It was all work, very hard and often dangerous, but it was work and people were glad to have a job, almost any job.

Back to Our Story

I remember the man in my story was always on the corner along with many others on the day the Relief Truck arrived, but I seldom saw him anywhere else in town. He seemed to be very much a home person. I often wondered why he met the relief truck and didn't send someone else. I sometimes stood on the corner or by the back of the truck and watched them fill the bags. Soon the bags contained a virtual horde of goodies. Some I was sure was undeserved, now I do not know that to be true; however, to me many seemed perfectly capable of working.

Homemade Projects

In my memory, the man worked on a number of minor projects. Were they inventions that he thought might make him rich? I didn't know. But even I knew that most of them were for his entertainment and a justification for not doing something more meaningful in life.

I believe his crowning achievement was the invention of what I now call the "fly zapper". It was an attempt at single fly execution without a fly swatter. I admit that flies were a problem in those summer days of long ago. There were few really operable screen doors and even if there were doors, many windows were without screens. If there were screens, they often had holes that were plenty big enough for a fly to crawl through and most flies found these holes easily. Not only were flies a carrier of germs; but they were an absolute nuisance.

It may have, in its original concept, seemed like a reasonable approach to an acute problem. Soon construction for this brainstorm was underway. Scrap materials were easily accessible in those days. Cheese came in a wooden box with wooden ends approximately four by four inches and the box was twelve to fourteen inches long. Their sides were only an eighth of an inch thick, four inches wide, and twelve to fourteen inches long. These boxes were good building materials.

You could, by carefully extraction, save the nails to be used again. The local grocery store was a virtual supply house for the "would be" crafter. Wooden boxes and crates came in weekly and were often not used again. The merchants were more than happy to give them away. They found their way into toy airplanes, boats, wooden guns, and boxes to hold all sorts of wonderful thing to play with. The novice inventor could also use them.

Faulty Design

I knew nothing about his designs, except this one. It was in a wooden box about twelve or fourteen inches long and about two or three inches deep. It had copper wires strung across the box and fastened at both ends. The wires extended beyond and were hitched to another wire that furnished the power. I knew neither about the power source or the fine details of the craftsmanship. I do not know whether he had electricity or had rigged one of those old fashion coils that came in a wooden box. They could deliver quite an electrical jolt when supplied with a DC current.

The object of this device was to get a housefly to light on one of the cross wires, and when he did, he was promptly executed. However, there was nothing to attract flies to the box, so the attraction was supplied. White syrup or molasses was put into the bottom of the box to attract the flies. It wasn't automatic; someone had to be there to throw a switch each time a fly was in position. It seemed like a lot of work to me and it required a great deal of patience.

I do remember that only a very few flies flew to their death on that box. In fact, the greatest problem was attracting these flies. I watched the efforts and was extremely disappointed. An old fashioned fly swatter worked much better. Fly swatters were not plastic in those days; in fact those were the days before plastic was in common use. The store bought swatters were made of screen wire on a wire handle. The homemade ones were usually made of a piece of rubber tire or inter tube fastened on a hickory stick handle, or possibly made of the soft leather of a shoe on the same type of handle.

The great fly zapper was a dismal failure, too many problems and too few flies. Soon it was discarded for another summer project. He never invented anything, but I think he had a lot of fun trying.

Don't Make Fun of Mother

A Short Story by Dr. Harry E. Carr

A Story Momma Told

Somewhere living in the memory of mother was this story. It seems there was a family that consisted of only a mother and three boys, the father was dead. The family probably lived somewhere in the hollar or beyond. Mother never told me where the story took place; it may have been a story that her mother had told her.

The Family

The widowed mother struggled to raise the boys by herself. In those days, there was no government agency to help families that were struggling. They usually counted on relatives or neighbors to help out, but everybody was expected to work.

Evening would find chores to be done, hogs to be fed, cows to be milked, eggs to be gathered, and the chickens to be fed. Everyone from the smallest up could do something. There was wood to bring in from the wood yard, a place where logs and poles were pulled up by the horses or hauled in by the wagon. Here they would wait to be cut into proper length for either the stove in the kitchen or the one that warmed the whole house in the living room. In both summer and winter, there were wood boxes to fill. Of course, there was no need for wood in the living room in the summer but the kitchen stove demanded much. It had to be dry. A common practice was to fill the cooling oven with wood for tomorrow, to dry or season it out a bit.

A Woman of Godly Character

The woman had earned a repetition in the community for her hard work providing for her family. She had raised her sons to be like her, godly, mannerly, kind, and hard working. They could usually find extra work in the summer chopping out the weeds from the corn or helping in the hay fields or the harvest fields. In the spring, they could plow with any man.

School

School consisted of only the first few grades and sometimes they were never finished. Most of the boys did well to have a fifth or sixth grade education. Education took place in a one-room school often miles away and there was no transportation so the children walked. The roads were safe in those days.

Taking The Strain Off Mother

The older the boys became the less her work became, for they could do a man's work in the field, and they brought their money home to support the family. In the process of raising her family, the mother had become old. Her back was bent, her hair was gray, and her steps had grown slow. From childhood, her sons were taught to obey and respect her. She was proud of them and they were deeply respectful of their mother.

Country Square Dances

Where there were country-dance floors, there were rowdy crowds, drinking, and fights. There might have been fights even had there not been liquor, but it was ever present. There was both the store bought kind purchased at the tavern at the county seat, and of course, the ever present "bootleg" whiskey made in some remote valley hidden from the eyes of the Revenuer. It showed up in fruit jars, gallon jugs, or in any kind of container that it wouldn't eat through.

The square dances sounded loud with the fiddles, guitars, and sometimes banjos. All went well until someone, usually with too much to drink, was offended then it was fists, knives, or guns. It was on a rare occasion that someone was killed. They were mostly just bruised or cut up. Usually the law was never called except on rare occasions and most had melted away into the night before the sheriff arrived.

The Wayward Boys

Now the boys had reached the age that they wanted to go to these dances. Mother objected to their going, but they were determined and went against her wishes. The next morning when the Mother started to reprimand them, they just held her and laughed. She didn't say a word but heart broken just walked away.

You're Not to Old for a Spanking

Those were the old-fashioned days, when discipline was expected and given. The boys felt that the days of discipline were long passed and now there would be none for sure. If mother tried, they would just simply hold her until she cooled off.

The day passed and suppertime came. The boys were at the supper table, but the conversation never got around to the events of the night before. They were too embarrassed to talk about it and they sure didn't plan on leaving home tonight.

Bedtime

Bedtime came and the boys turned in, they all slept together in an old-fashioned high-posted straw bed. Mother waited until they were all sound asleep, then she quietly took the two sheets and stitched them tightly together over the sleeping boys.

A lightweight frying pan made a good paddle, and she let each one of them have a few sharp smacks. They were surprised, confused, and a bit scared. The sheets were stitched so tightly that they could hardly move.

She did not leave her boys all sewed up for the night, but cut the sheets loose right away. The boys, thoroughly humiliated and ashamed, were filled with deep consternation. With hugs and kisses, they embraced their little mother. Each made their own deep apologies and sincere promises to a mother who loved them all dearly. Never again did they mock their mother. Each boy later married and raised their own family with the same deep religious convictions that they had themselves been raised by.

They often laughed, so I am told, about the night mother took her revenge. I image that they repeated it to their children on many occasions.

I never knew whether Mother told me the story just to remind me that I wasn't getting too big to be spanked, or if it actually happened as she told it. I may have been trying to assert my imaginary grown up status and mother used the story to remind me that you never get too big to be disciplined by a loving parent.

It is true that Mother sometimes liked to illustrate her strongest views with a good story or a very positive statement like, "if you do that you are going to get hurt." I soon learned that the things that I might do were not always the way I got hurt. It usually came as the result of a handy peach tree limb in Momma's hand.

To me this story just became one of the stories of Momma's childhood in the "hollar".

The Last Batch of Sorghum Molasses

A Short Story by Dr. Harry E. Carr

A Boy Remembers

As with all stories, I will tell this story from a boy's eyewitness account. Everything will be told as only a boy saw it. It has been more than sixty years ago and I am sure that some details will be fuzzy and some will appear bigger than they really were, but I think it is a story worth telling. So get some butter and hot biscuits and we will enjoy a plate of molasses together.

Syrup

You could, even in those days, buy Karo syrup. It was thick and came in two flavors, a kind of maple and vanilla. I personally did not like either flavor, besides it was too thick to soak up in a biscuit. This syrup cost more money than sorghum and we usually could ill afford to spend it. We did not have maple syrup, although I am sure it was available but it cost even more than the Karo brand.

All the syrup we had came in two varieties. "Sugar Lasses" which was sugar and water cooked down into a light syrup. It was good on biscuits in the morning, but it took a lot of sugar to make, and sugar was another one of those things we did not raise or could not make. It too must be purchased. Of course, the other syrup was sorghum. We tried to make enough to last all winter. By late spring or early summer, the syrup was turning to sugar. The trick in trying to reconstitute it was to put it into a pan of water and bring the water to a boil. The heated syrup would gradually lose its granular taste and become syrup again.

Other Uses for Sorghum

In the wintertime, sorghum was good for many things. You could make sorghum taffy, which was very tasty and very chewy. It was boiled until when dropped into cold water it quickly formed into a ball. Cooled, it was coated with flour and pulled. It was such a fun thing to do on long cold winter nights. You could also heat it and make popcorn balls. When the popcorn was rolled in the syrup, it stuck together.

They were not only good to eat, but you could also use them for Christmas tree ornaments.

Sorghum and a Long Winter

A winter without sorghum was long and boring. Of course, we usually had some type of fruit for breakfast, but a big family can go through a lot of black berries and peaches in those cold months. Peach juice poured over a biscuit crust made a delectable finish to a breakfast of bacon, sausage, ham, or pork shoulder that had been fried with gravy made from the drippings.

Of course, there was always plenty of homemade "from scratch" biscuits. Coffee and tea were the breakfast drinks and milk for the young. Grandpa never drank coffee on any occasion; it was always black tea. It was brewed by boiling it in an old teapot that used only tea grounds. He drank it at every meal, usually hot and without cream or sugar, except in the summer, then he would give way to ice tea for the dinner and supper meals. He would drink the tea and then it was as if he felt he had some in each corner of his handle bar mustache, so he would retrieve it by nibbling on the end of his mustache.

Sorghum was not reserved just for breakfast; it appeared on the table at almost every meal. However, if you ate it for dinner or supper, you probably had to eat it with cornbread. It wasn't too bad, but it was much better with biscuits.

Where Do You Get Sorghum?

You could usually buy sorghum at the local stores in town. It was always a little higher in price, so we either made it ourselves or bought it from another sorghum mill. There was a secret to cooking sorghum. You did not want it too green or too dark, the one way it was under cooked and the other way it was over cooked. It took real skill to get it just right. Some people developed a reputation for good sorghum.

Of course, we did not make sorghum just for our own use; Daddy made it so that he would have a few extra buckets to sell to neighbors and friends. To my knowledge, there were no local regulations on the making of sorghum. I believe that Dad and Grandpa both had a reputation for good sorghum and it was easy to sell every bucket that we did not need for our own use.

The finished molasses was drained into four or eight-pound syrup buckets and sealed with the metal lid. The new bright syrup buckets glimmered in the bright summer sun. We usually had some buckets left over from last year and new buckets could be bought at the local hardware store during sorghum time.

The Last Patch of Cane

The last batch of sorghum cane that I remember working on was raised in the creek bottom just east of Hosick Creek. The field was not large, only a few acres, but big enough to make several gallons of sorghum. To the casual glance, sorghum cane looked a lot like corn when it was growing. It required rich ground and lots of water, thus making a creek bottom an ideal place for its growth.

Since we didn't own the property, I assume that we raised the cane on the shares. I learned the sad lesson that in those days the owner got a third of the harvest by just owning the property. He did none of the work, had no expense in buying the seed, nor did he help in the harvest. I thought the job of the landowner must be the way to go, but we didn't own any land much less a farm.

Growing the Cane for the Mill

I think the hardest job of all was the final steps in the harvest. Plowing the field and preparing it for seeding was hard, but it moved along well and even the seeding went well. The new stalks had to be plowed and the weeds cut out with a hoe. This was only difficult when the stalks were neck high to a boy. The leaves would leave scratch marks on your arms and neck that would smart with the sweat of a hot summer day. I hated chopping out corn and it was the same in the cane fields.

"Stripping" the Cane

In the late summer, when the sorghum cane was about five feet tall, it was full-grown. Now the work really began. The mill and cooking pan had to be moved in and set. The rollers and the trough leading to the cooking pan were in place and the rollers were ready for the sorghum canes.

Workers had to go into the fields and strip the cane of all their blades, leaving the sorghum cane stalks standing like skeletons in the summer sun. Once the field was all stripped, it was time to cut the cane and haul it to the mill.

Soon sled loads of cane were taken across the creek and to the mill.

The Sorghum Mill

The sorghum mill consisted of only two things. The first was a device for extracting juice from the cane. This was two grooved cylinders that rolled together squeezing the cane between them. A single horse or mule pulled a pole in a wide circle, powering the mill. The second was a copper cooking pan with dividers and a wooden hoe.

The mill sat close to the ground and the pole pulled by the horse or mule was not far off the ground either, perhaps three feet, unless it was put up on blocks to make to make it higher. To feed the cane into the mill you must either be short or nearly lay down. Usually the smallest persons were selected to feed the mill. The juice flowed from the rollers down a trough leading to the cooking pan.

The Cooking Pan

The mill had been set on the west side of the creek near the gravel road that joined the state route three quarters of a mile away. Stones and blocks were put under the pan to keep it off the ground. Wood was gathered for the fire. It was important to keep a constant temperature under the pan or the sorghum would not cook properly.

The pan was separated by wooden partitions. One partition joined one end, and the next partition joined the other end, creating a maze. The juice would come into the front of the pan and the cooker would slowly move it towards the end of the pan giving it proper cooking time. The smell of cooking sorghum was one of the greatest smells of summer. The sorghum would foam up in the pan, and the cooker with his wooden hoe would skim off the foam, discarding it by the pan. The foam crystallized and was sweet and pleasant to the taste, but it could not be cooked into the molasses.

The Cooking Begins

Piled up behind the rollers were stacks of sorghum cane. The horse or mule was hitched to the rollers and began the monotonous task of walking in a circle, supplying power to the rollers. The feeder began to run the cane between the rollers, and soon the sweet syrup was running in a steady stream into the pan.

Coordinating the Cooking

The cooker was in charge. If the syrup came to fast, he would slow down the feeder. The fire had to be kept at a proper heat, which required one man or boy to keep it going. Slowly the molasses moved down the pan, reaching at last, the place where others were waiting to fill the buckets. It was tasted again and again. It must be just right. Whatever we did as a family had to be the best we could do. Nothing less ever suited either Grandpa or Dad.

A Great Summer

I said it was a great summer. I don't know how many buckets we made or how many we sold. I just enjoyed the cooking, smelling, and eating. There were full buckets and people came and bought them. There would be molasses and some extra money for the other things a family would need. But best of all, we had done it together as a family. Everybody worked and there were few complaints.

Somewhere people have lost the idea of working together to meet the needs of the family. We have also, somewhere along the way, lost the pride of a finished product in which we could have family pride.

The Last Summer of Sorghum Making

This would be the last summer of molasses making for our family. Somehow the copper pan developed a hole and we were not able to fix it. Frankly, I was disappointed. There was no explanation given, the mill was just discarded, the cane was not planted, and sorghum making came to an end.

Maybe I am just nostalgic, but I missed those days of sorghum cooking, the bright shining buckets and the smell of cooking syrup. I still eat sorghum occasionally, when I can find a good bucket or jar.

I know that I am prejudice; however, I have never found a bucket of sorghum as good as those made along Hosick Creek long ago and far away.

Two Boys and a BB Gun

A Short Story by Dr. Harry E. Carr

A BB Gun

Like all farm boys, I longed to own a genuine Daisy Red Ryder BB gun. Daisy had a number of different air rifles differing in appearance, the number of BBs the magazine would hold, and the way they operated. There was the cheapest, it was shorter than the others and loaded by breaking the stock down away from the barrel. It held one BB at a time, which had to be dropped in the barrel before the gun was actually loaded. Somehow, this held the BB in place, at least most of the time. It was also the most modest priced available, but it was still way out of our price range.

Don't Ask For Too Much

I would have had better luck asking for all the tea in China than asking for even this poor little BB gun for Christmas. I just didn't ask for any big things in those days, we knew to keep our requests small and reasonable. Money in those days was always scarce and it seemed, at least to me, that it was scarcer at Christmas than at any other time. I was always concerned at Christmas time. It seemed like that was the time of year when work was scarce or the mines were laying off. It was indeed bad to be broke with Christmas coming.

Birthday Celebration

We did not get gifts on birthdays. Sometimes we would have a homemade cake, usually without candles, but it was still a treat. I especially liked Grandma or Mom's cake that was made from "scratch". It was usually a yellow cake with white nearly candied icing. Grandma boiled milk, sugar, vanilla, and I never knew what else on the stove. It was thin when it was applied to the cake, but when it cooled, it usually broke when cutting the cake. A fellow could flake the icing off and eat the bare cake later.

You'll Shoot Yourself in the Eye Theory

Every mother had this fear. I suppose that it actually happened somewhere sometime, but I neither knew the place, the time, or anyone who had actually been shot in the eye. Admittedly, it was possible, but not if you had any respect for a gun. It wasn't like you would look down the barrel of a loaded gun while asking your brother to try the trigger.

The Only Way To Own A BB Gun

We already carried some formidable weapons - our slingshots. They were a forked stock with two strong rubber bands and a shoe tongue for a pouch. They could bring down a frog or a small animal. We were allowed only to shoot at the former or at a snake. They were fair game anywhere.

There was a seed company in Pennsylvania that offered a Daisy Red Rider BB gun as a prize for selling garden and flower seeds. It would be impossible to sell enough seed to get the gun in one year, but maybe I could do it in two.

I certainly never thought that I was a salesman; however if the prize was worthwhile, I would certainly try. Christmas had come and gone, with the usual medal truck made out to Jake and I, and sometimes it was made out to our sister Helen as well. I thought that Santa Clause was pretty dumb. I never noticed my name on her doll and I certainly did not want it there, but why in the world would a girl want to have a third of an interest in a metal truck.

There was often some sort of game for all. One year it was a "Uncle Wiggly" game, another year it was Chinese checkers because six could play. But mostly we used a homemade "Fox and Geese" gameboard or an old set of checkers.

Great Plans

I knew there would be no BB gun under the Christmas tree; however, I did get permission to order the garden and flower seed. It was a nickel or a dime per package and everyone needed garden seed. During the early spring, I managed to sell all of that shipment and ordered another. It did not go as well and I never finished selling all of it until the winter months.

The money had been sent to the seed company. I would try to sell a third box in the early spring. I was able to sell everything but some of the flower seed, which I had to return; however, there had been enough. I had earned that new 250 shot Red Rider Daisy BB gun.

Watching the Mail

Soon we would have a BB gun. I didn't think of anything much apart from Jake. We were the joint-owners of all our toys. I guess we both longed for something that could be just our own, but we knew that we must share everything. I guess I just never really resented that.

We both would walk the half-mile to the mailbox every day to check on the BB gun. A week passed and still it wasn't here and then another came and went. What was taking them so long? Had they quit making the gun? Had some mother convinced them that they should quit BB guns and protect the eyes of the American boys? Did I not send in enough money? Maybe I had failed to send in the right things. While you wait, a thousand questions ply your mind making you wonder.

A BB Gun In The Mail

Despite all my worries and concerns, the gun arrived in the mail. It came in a long cardboard box with the figure of Red Ryder on the outside. The wooden stock engraved with the name of a western hero was varnished in a walnut color of brown and the long blue shiny barrel was waiting to be used. There was even a leather strap in the ring near the stock. It was just perfect, there was only one thing missing, the BBs.

We would have to wait until we went to town to buy BBs. They came in a tube of one hundred and cost a nickel. We didn't have the opportunity to go to town and I certainly didn't have a nickel. We would just have to wait. In the meantime, we polished the gun, practiced using it, and waited for that time when we would finally get a tub of BBs.

A Serious Lesson Learned

We finally had our BBs and found ways to conserve them. If you put a target on a heavy cardboard box, the BBs would not penetrate the box. We could dig the BBs out with our knife and use them again and again. All you needed was the strength to pull up the handle and you were ready to shoot. We had a great time sharing that air rifle.

Sometimes we would divide the BBs between the two of us. Each would have a turn to shoot his share of the BBs. Of course, whoever had the biggest pile kept the gun the most, and each tried to conserve the BBs.

I was the oldest so I divided the BBs, and being a boy with a boy's nature, I gave myself all the advantages. I was all of eight years old at the time. Jake stood by while I made the division, holding the loaded BB gun. I was piling the BBs on two separate pieces of paper, although Jake did not count very well at the time, he knew enough to recognize that he had the smaller pile. He expressed his deep disapproval by shooting me in the hand. It was not a serious wound, but I am sure I made the most out of it.

The first words from Mom were, "See I told you one of you would get shot." But this was no accident; the gun did not discharge accidentally, although Jake was prepared to swear it did. He wasn't anxious for the spanking, but I longed to see him get it. It wasn't much of a spanking, Mother's spankings never were. My lecture about proper division lasted much longer than his spanking, besides I was, in my estimation, severely wounded and bleeding profusely.

I really learned something that day. "You mean you learned to keep the piles of BBs near the same size, or to divide equally, or to be fair." No, sorry to disappoint you. What I really learned was never to divide BBs while your younger brother held a loaded air rifle and was watching the division. That could be dangerous.

A Nose Ring for a Black Angus Bull

A Short Story by Dr. Harry E. Carr

Going Back Home

It is always good to return to the old home place, if it is nothing more than empty buildings or lots where the buildings used to be. There are memories waiting to be discovered and relived in your mind, and to be shared with the next generation who is running around the barn lot making memories of their own.

My family and I had taken a church in Michigan nearly six hundred miles from my last home place. Although I was sure this was the will of God for our family, I still missed home and the family very much and welcomed every opportunity to spend a few days with Dad and Mom.

Down on the Farm

There were a thousand places that brought back memories, although the house that was there now was not the one in which I spend my last teen years. The old house was a four-room log house with a lean to in the back for a kitchen. The old wood stove had put out many meals for our kitchen table during those last years of high school.

A Road in the Wilderness

Occasionally I would walk up the lane toward the distant back woods. Dad only owned a strip sixteen rods wide and a quarter mile long; it opened into his back forty-acre field. When we purchased the farm with the access strip, the strip was all heavy forested with mostly large oak trees. Many of those were cut down and sent to the sawmill to make lumber for a barn. However, those along the creek and the hill were left.

Two large limestone rocks made a natural cooking pit. It was a great place to cook whatever we could find at home. Here we spend many a summer day. We drank the water from the spring branch; it was far too cold to swim in had there been a hole deep enough.

The Far Back Woods

The back woods were my joy. They were a great place to hunt, wander, or to just think. It had plenty of squirrels and other wild game. There were four trees that were my favorites. One was a large hickory that was just after you entered the woods. It had a beehive in the upper part, but I never told anyone that I knew it was there. The second was the old hickory that sat deep in the woods; it always had hickory nuts in the fall. They were much too hard to crack and the kernel was small, but the squirrels really loved that tree. If there was a squirrel in that section of the woods, you could bet that he would be on that tree. The third was a large sassafras tree that had a large beehive in it. We cut it down shortly after we bought the farm. The last was a fallen tree; the old log on the ground was full of honey.

Jake and I had started a cabin on the back creek bank. We sawed and set the poles in the ground, but never finished the cabin. Dad found the poles set firmly in the ground and often speculated about those four posts, but neither Jake nor I ever told him why they were there.

There was the strawberry patch at the entrance of the woods, where I picked a few messes of strawberries in season. They were extremely small but very good; a few could flavor a cake very well. An old roadway from many years gone by ran along the edge of the field. It was a great place to slip up on squirrels, but far too overgrown to travel.

The Barn and Feeding Time

Memories lived everywhere. They were in the barn where we fed and milked the cows; Jake always did the milking while I fed the hogs. Of course, feeding the hogs seemed a lot easier to me. The hill from the barn sloped away to the water hole. A woven wire fence with two strands of barbwire ran down the property line of our farm. It too had special memories. Here one stormy afternoon, I was milking the cows for Dad and Mom because they were on vacation, when a summer thunderstorm came up quickly.

A Lightening Strike

My wife, Alberta, was leaning on the fence watching me finish with the milking, when a bolt of lightning struck the fence, several hundred yards away. The old fence was well into the ground and ran underwater in the big water hole. Nevertheless, some of the voltage got through and followed the wires down to where Alberta was. Of course most of the high voltage had entered the ground at the strike and more of it along the way, still she got a heavy shock that knocked her back on her heels. Her arm was numb for a while, but otherwise she was ok. However, this left a lasting memory, at least for Alberta.

A Baby Hawk

One morning I entered the woods and heard a baby hawk squawking. It was still very dark and I could not find him. I finished my hunt and on the way home, I stopped again. Most of the trees were far to small for a hawk's nest so where in the world did that baby hawk come from? Then I found him, in a box nailed on a tree. My younger brother had brought him home and mom was trying to feed him oats and cracked corn. I picked up the hawk and carried him to the house and called for Mom. "Mom, hawks eat meat. They don't eat grain."

On a diet of meat and fish, he grew into a beautiful bird. Fully grown, my brother released him again into the wild. Hawks ought to be free, hunting the fields and woods and riding on the winds. I love to hear their hunting cry, which brings mice, snakes, and small rabbits scurrying to see and all too often becoming a hawk's next meal.

Some Memories of the Barn

Many changes had been made, but despite the changes all things seem to be the same. The old barn still stood with memories that resisted the passing of time.

My son David might tell the story of the white roosters. Mother had bought a dozen or so roosters for us at a farm auction. She had shut them up in the hallway of the barn and fattened them up for the time that we would be home on vacation.

What would we do with all those fat roosters? We would kill and dress the rooster and freeze it for the long trip back to

Michigan. They would make great chicken and dumplings for the family.

This morning Mom and my wife, Alberta, had heated the water to scald the rooster for plucking and dressing, while David and I went to the barn to kill the rooster and get them ready to dress. I always shot chickens on the farm as a boy growing up. Mom would simply describe the chicken she wanted and I would take my 22-caliber rifle, shoot the bird through the head, and bring it back to her. I prefer shooting the birds to wringing their necks. So off went David and I to the barn and I was carrying the rifle.

Now shooting a rooster in the head with a 22 is not an easy thing to do. However, one by one, I killed the roosters. They were ready for plucking and we headed to the house. I thought David would be impressed with my shooting; however, his comment to his mother was not about my skill but about my one miss. "Daddy missed on one of the roosters and had to shoot twice." "Thanks David, what about the others I did not miss?" There was no comment, most boys at that age think Daddy does things perfect every time.

When we are growing up, we seldom think about all the good times we are having, but the memory recalls them sometimes at the most unexpected moments. It is good to stop and listen again for the sound of an old Fordson tractor whining in the back field, the sound of animals as they settle down for the night, to hear Mom's call to supper, and to live again the experiences of a boyhood long past but never forgotten.

Putting a Ring in the Bull's Nose

I wandered again past the elm tree that stood by the road down near the waterhole. It is a lot larger now, but in those days, it was only about a foot in diameter. It reminded me of an incident of long ago. I was home on vacation, when Dad said, "Son would you help me put a ring in the bull's nose today." Of course, I said, "Yes" without giving it a thought.

I saw him down at the barn, he was a little Black Angus bull but little was a bad estimation. That bull weighed at least six or seven hundred pounds, maybe even more. He seemed passive enough, even friendly. He was short, black, and stout. Dad came with a nose ring and fifty foot of strong rope. The ring was one that just clamped on and did not require the nose to be punched. A bull's nose is a very sensitive area.

Holding the Rope

Dad fastened the rope, of all places, to the bull's halter. I sure wished it had been a chokehold. I took two wraps around that elm tree; it should have been four, five, or six wraps to give me more leverage. I backed up, put the rope around my hips, wrapped it around my hands, and set my feet. I was ready, at least, I thought I was ready.

Everything was going just fine, until Dad started putting the ring in the bull's nose, to which Mr. Bull objected strenuously. He lunged against the rope so strongly that his front feet came off the ground. Dad was older now and did not move as fast as he used to, and that bull hit him, knocking him sprawling.

I thought I could stop him, but he was pulling that rope through my hands. If I let go, the bull would, at the least, trample Dad. I had my mind made up, that bull was not going to get on my Dad. My heels were dug in but the rope was slipping, I gripped it tighter. I could feel the rope burning the palms of my hands, but I would not let go. Why, because Dad wasn't yet out of the way. As soon as he was safely away, I turned loose. By that time, I had severe burns and the hide was gone in some places. But the bull never got to Dad.

I thought of Dad again today as I wrote. You see back then, I didn't see the slowing of his steps. I didn't see him getting old until that day. It only made me love him more.

Love makes us do some unusual things and gives us a strength that we never dreamed we had. I never said a word about my rope burned hands to Daddy, he found out later. I just went back to the house for bandages. We didn't get the ring in the bull's nose until we had more help, but he did wear the ring. You see, Dad too was a very determined man.

My Last Horseback Ride with Grandpa

A Short Story by Dr. Harry E. Carr

No Baking Powder

I had been working with Grandpa all morning in the fields, and when we came in at noon Granny announced that she was out of meal and baking powder. She could neither make cornbread or biscuits. There were many things that Grandpa would do without, but bread was not one of them. It was imperative that we always had some type of meat and bread on the table for every meal.

It was the way he was raised and the way he raised his family. Meat consisted of fresh or salt pork or chicken. Beef was out of the question and I was told that we did not like turkey or goose. I agreed with the idea of not eating one of the geese, they always seemed too fat and oily to eat. But turkey was another question, and I never quite understood why we didn't eat one.

Why We Never Cooked Turkeys

So one day I asked Granny why she never fixed a turkey. I knew we had them, I had watched them enough growing up. Watched them? Yes, you see, even in a tame turkey, there is something of the wild turkey instincts. When nesting time came, they did not lay their eggs at the hen house or barn, they would slip away and lay their eggs in some hidden place somewhere in the edge of the woods, deep in the brush or under a brush pile. Granny wanted them found and brought in, lest some skunk, raccoon, or chicken snake would find them and eat or destroy the whole nest. Sometimes she would put a small turkey bell on their necks. I believe they could hold the clapper on that bell. I would be watching, waiting for her to go to the nest and suddenly, I would look away and the turkey was gone.

Well Granny finally answered my question. "I fixed a turkey once and nobody would eat it. We don't like turkeys." That was that and she didn't ever fix another one. With Granny, I dared venture another question. How did you fix the turkey? When I learned that she had boiled it, I agreed that nobody liked it. At our house, meat was boiled or fried, very seldom was it baked. But why she choose to boil a turkey, I couldn't imagine. Was she going to make "turkey and dumplings"? I do know she makes the greatest chicken and dumplings I have ever ate. There was a dumpling special that I loved most of all. She also made black berry dumplings; it makes my mouth water just to think of them. I haven't had any in years, but I would be tempted to walk home just to get a pot of those dumplings.

Breakfast at Grandma's House

Now boiled turkey probably quenches your appetite as well as mine. A fat hen or rooster, that was different. For breakfast, pork, ham, and shoulder meat were eaten first and then came the bacon. It had been cured with white salt and stored in a huge meat box. The months past and the meat became stronger and stronger in taste and was difficult to eat. Grandpa seemed to have no trouble eating the meat at all. Occasionally I would try a little bit; it wasn't too bad if you hid it in a biscuit or a fair size chunk of cornbread. We did, on occasion when the frying chickens were first coming on in the spring, have fried chicken for breakfast. Now that might sound unappetizing to you, but with white gravy, biscuits, and potatoes it was mighty good for any meal.

The Trip to the Store

Grandpa decided that we would have go to the store. It was six or seven miles away and Grandpa did not have a car. He never owned one and never drove one. Well, I should take that back, Daddy said he tried once. He was frustrated and would have wrecked if Daddy hadn't been with him to stop the car. He never tried to drive a car again; he stuck with what he knew best, the horse and wagon.

Transportation

We went to the barn and caught Fred; a blazed faced, stocking footed sorrel, one of the most beautiful horses Grandpa owned. I was to ride Charlie. He was a bay with a dark mane and tail. He was half Morgan and half quarter horse. He was the fastest horse we had for the first quarter of a mile and after that he could and would be passed. He was the most hypertensious horse I ever knew. Speak to him sharply and he was nervous for the rest of the day.

He also had a very bad habit. When you started to mount him from the left side, as soon as your foot hit the stirrup and your backside was stretched out, he would take a bite out of your rump. We knew this, so we always pull Charlie's head as far to the right as possible, and with the reins held tight you made a quick clean mount. You dared not bobble or bounce to mount or you were in serious trouble. As soon as the unsuspecting rider sunk his foot in the stirrup, Charlie sprung into action. We, who were familiar with Charlie, never warned the unknowing of this particular quirk of his. It was more fun watching them learn life's lesson by experience.

We owned only two saddles one was a McClellan, which Grandpa used because it was the bigger of the two saddles. (The "McClellan" saddle was a creation of General McClellan from the Civil War era. It had a smooth bow without a saddle horn.) I do admit that this is a good saddle for breaking a horse. (A saddle horn can have a disastrous effect if the horse throws you up into the air.) The other saddle was a smaller Texas saddle, which I used.

Leaving the Barn

Soon the horses were saddled and we were on our way to town. I was having a pleasant day with Grandpa. We had just turned out of the barn lot and started down the long and very steep Raines Hill towards Three-Mile Creek, when not fifty yards down the hill, Charley shied hard to the right. Not expecting the sudden move, I nearly toppled from the saddle right in the middle of a big snake. I had been riding on the left edge of the road (on a gravel road, the edge is always grassy) and suddenly I was over in the right track nearly hitting Grandpa. Then I saw it, a large Copper head, which is a type of the pit viper, was coiled ready to strike. He was right where we had been. Charley had just barely missed getting bitten by the snake. I was very early in my teen years, but I already knew what to do with snakes. Dismounting at a safe distance and armed with the largest rocks I could find, I took care of the snake while Grandpa looked on with approval.

The Store of Choice

We could have probably found the items Grandma needed at the small store at Stone Church, however, Grandpa wanted to go to Henry's store in Elizabethtown. Wherever Grandpa wanted to go that is where we went, no questions asked and no argument made.

It was a pleasant trip; we never know when we are going to make the last ride together. Make each one pleasant, for they will be the memory of years to come. The trip went without any other incident. In Henry's store, the purchases were made. The pop sure looked good and so did the candy, but I did not get either. Money was scarce and we did not waste it on pop and candy. I remember the smell of the store and the sight of the goods, but I wasn't too disappointed because I wasn't use to having those things anyway. With the groceries slung across the saddle, we headed home. It was late afternoon when we climbed back up the long hill toward the barn.

Home Again

It would soon be feeding and milking time and supper was not too far away. There would be cornbread on the table along with the other things Grandma always seemed to know how to especially prepare. One more time, we would sit down at the table and Grandpa would bow his white head and pray, "O Lord, we thank thee," and from there on there was not a single word of his prayer that I could understand until he got to his final Amen. Still yet, God was a part of our life, every day and at every meal.

Memories

Years have gone, but that last ride lives in my memory and in my heart. Grandpa was a stern old man, absolutely honest and trustworthy. No one could work harder or longer than he could. But I suspect, that he had a bit of a soft spot and a smile behind that tough handle bar mustache. More than anyone ever dreamed, I believe he liked having someone to ride with him, and I am glad I was the one.